JUDGE
THIS
COVER

BY
BRITTANY RENNER

Library of Congress Cataloging-in-Publication Data
Brittany Renner
Judge This Cover
Published by: B. Renner Fitness

ISBN: 978-0692156506
10 9 8 7 6 5 4 3 2 1
Printed in the United States of America

Note: This book is intended only as a real life testimony of the life and times of Brittany Renner. Readers are advised to consult a professional before making any changes in their life. The reader assumes all responsibility for the consequences of any actions taken based on the information presented in this book. The information in this book is based on the author's experiences. Every attempt has been made to ensure that the information is accurate; however, the author cannot accept liability for any errors that may exist. The facts and theories about life are subject to interpretation, and the conclusions and recommendations presented here may not agree with other interpretations.

TABLE OF CONTENTS

DEDICATION

On the days I felt like giving up and not finishing this book I thought of you. Not knowing when I'll see you again makes me sad and blue, but when the sunshine greets me in the morning I know it's you. Dedicated to my sweet Grams like I promised that night at Red Lobster...

Dear Reader,

My name is Brittany Renner and the first time I ever felt passionate about anything was when I decided to write a book at age 25. Who knew IG thots have the mental capacity to read and write? Baffling, *isn't it?* This story is my unmasked truth. Regardless of how you interpret what you're about to read, I am not sorry now nor will I ever apologize for my feelings. I am entitled to my feelings - good, bad, or indifferent - all while still knowing, at any point in time, they may evolve and change. I choose to proudly stand by my emotions even when they fail to be politically correct. The truth is not always glamorous, but it shouldn't have to be.

This is my story of seven men and seven lessons, all based on true events. There is no denying that I cared about all seven men you will come to know, each for their own unique reasons. To pretend their roles didn't impact my life would be a slap in the face to the knowledge I inherited. You can't regret a person you once used to "sweat." I've made naughty videos, sent shameless paragraphs, and a few heated voice texts that would make for great song intros. I came, I saw it wasn't what I thought it would be, I learned, and I conquered. The names in this book will remain undisclosed, for my revenge is artistic, not personal.

I shed countless tears throughout my entire writing process. No matter how much time passes, you never forget the way someone made you feel. Reliving painful memories I once buried so deep and tried so hard to forget opened my eyes to the pain I hoarded in the crevices of my heart. As an individual who sees a therapist weekly,

I'm 100% committed to my mental health, despite being often labeled as crazy. Crazy doesn't think they need help or want help. Crazy would never make the conscious effort towards self-betterment day in and day out. The deeper I dove into my writing, the more I was able to paint the picture of my pain in my therapy sessions. This acknowledgment of my wounds allowed me to simultaneously pull from the roots and heal. In order to move forward, you must be willing to travel back in time to where it all began. I knew I would never find balance in the denial of my darkness.

Once you're a presence on the internet, nothing is sacred. You will be judged for the most minute aspects of your life, such as needing a nail fill, to the most intimate and personal areas of your life, such as people talking shit about your family. Welcome to the World Wide Web where strangers know you better than you know yourself and everyone is seemingly perfect! No amount of money or stature exempts you from being dragged if the public catches you slipping. Perception is deception. It's never as good as it seems and it's never as bad as it seems because, well...nothing is ever as it seems. Life is one big ongoing joke that nobody is in on unless you're able to appreciate the humor in the irony. Like being tested on equations with an overpriced calculator you will never use outside of the classroom, but never learning the importance of empathy, healing, or owning what makes you special. You can bet your bottom dollar that you'll walk across that stage, smiling ear to ear with your degree in hand, without ever grasping the concept of time management, credit, and taxes. The education system gifts this nonsense as "everything you need to be prepared for the real world" and tops it with a cap and gown as the bright red bow. It is undeniably crystal clear that we are not prepared for the challenges of this cruel world. We are merely sheeple groomed to file in line.

At the end of the day, there will be people who take nothing away from the experiences in this book other than confirmation that I'm a scorned crazy bitch who outed seven men and is not to be trusted. Well, since some already think those things, and I don't give a single fuck, you're in luck! With silence, you can say absolutely nothing and still be siding with the oppressor. Where's the fun in conformity when the truth can set us all free? I firmly believe life would not be worth living if I ever had to live a lie. None of us can escape death, but the truth will live on forever.

INTRO

My name is Brittany Renner and I am 25 years old. I am originally from Ontario, Ohio but was raised the majority of my life in a small predominately white town called Ocean Springs, Mississippi. Whenever I explained to people what part of Mississippi I always said, "It's an hour from New Orleans." The majority of Americans couldn't locate it on a map, and even if they could, they most likely have never been there. There's not much going on in Ocean Springs besides soaring rates of teen pregnancy, obesity, and painfully slow customer service. It was a common occurrence to see big trucks used for mud riding with confederate flags waving behind them, symbolizing, "I call black people the n-word and I'm proud!" Things were a little slower down in the south, seeing how we ranked high in everything frowned upon except education. *Why do y'all think we talk the way we do?*

I have two brothers and one sister, but since my oldest brother has a different mother, we didn't meet until later in life. It was pretty awkward the first time we met, considering he tried to "big brother" me when I was the oldest amongst my two siblings. My mom never married, which was surprising since she always managed to prioritize men over us. She was the youngest and most rebellious of her two sisters. Growing up, she was naturally gifted in sports but never applied herself due to her obsession with black dick since she was a young teen. She birthed me at the tender age of 19 during a time when having a biracial child was considered shameful because of the blatant racism in America. My mom is one of those white girls who think she's black, and my dad is actually black. My mom's side of the family was so embarrassed that they weren't anywhere to be found in the delivery room when I was born. Thankfully, my grandma put her opinions to the side and came up to the hospital shortly after I arrived into the world on February 26, 1992. I didn't have the warmest of welcomes, but eventually, they all got over it and have loved me without question ever since.

My dad was an alcoholic who was always in and out of jail for drinking and driving, so he was never around. *Typical, right?* Girls without dads grow up to be the biggest whores because the first man who is supposed to love a young girl, doesn't. Isn't that how that narrative goes? We're in search of something, but we can't quite place our finger on exactly what it is because we've never had it.

After eight years of living with my mom in Ohio, she randomly asked all of us if we wanted to move to Mississippi where my grandparents lived. My grandparents left Ohio because my grandpa found a job with better pay in Mississippi. Of course, we said yes! What child doesn't love their grandparents who spoil them rotten? Little did we know, our mom didn't want to be a mom. She dropped us off at our grandparents' house and we only saw her when she'd occasionally pop in to say hello. She often promised us things like outings to the movies or the zoo, but she almost never followed through on these promises. Even as children, my siblings and I would give her chance after chance to prove that each time would be different from the last, but the change we wanted never came. That constant fear of disappointment is something I still grapple with as an adult. I never hope for anything with too much excitement. I keep those feelings of anticipation at bay as a way to protect my heart from disappointment. As children, we are burdened with this nagging curse of unconditional love that binds us to these people who created us no matter how much they hurt us. The yearning for their love is constant.

Around middle school age, I approached my grandma and asked her how we could contact my dad in jail. I loved my grandparents so much, but not knowing my dad always left me feeling like part of me was missing. My parents made the adult decision to lay down without the use of a condom, but neither of them had any interest in being parents. We got the address, and shortly after, I sent my father my first letter. I remember reading the few letters we exchanged, eyes wide open and filled with excitement to learn about this person who helped create me. I had a pen pal in school and this sort of felt like that. After he was released, I met my dad for the first time when I was fifteen years old. Although I was only a teenager, I felt like I didn't need a dad when I had made it that far without him. I knew I was half of him, but he didn't even know the half of me. I really needed my dad long before I ever met him.

My grandma's love was priceless, but also extremely strict and often times suffocating. She was superwoman; she got us ready for school, had dinner prepared by 5:30 pm, snack at 8:00 pm, and put us to bed at 9:00 pm every single night. Her rules provided the structure we needed to stay in line. Considering the fact that she didn't exactly sign up for this, I admired her greatly for her choice to step up for us in the name of love. She loved us all so much that she was willing to shelter us from the world rather than equip us for it. We weren't allowed to watch certain channels on television, grew up on country music, and she rarely let us go to hang out with friends. One would think that being raised by white people who acknowledged nothing of our blackness would leave anyone white-washed. Well, I was white-washed. Even though my grandparents said color never mattered, it definitely didn't stop the embarrassing remarks that came out of my grandma's mouth. No, the color of someone's skin doesn't make them lesser, but society tries to convince us otherwise.

During my earlier years in school, I was the type who cried when my car got moved from green to yellow for being "too talkative." I was - and still am - highly sensitive, but I always managed to stay out of trouble. I hated every minute of school. My grades weren't the best, but I maintained the bare minimum to be eligible for soccer. In sports, however, I didn't have to work hard to be great. I had no idea what I wanted to do with my life because I wasn't interested in much outside of soccer. I never quite understood how any person at a young age was expected to know what they wanted to do in life for the rest of their life with no actual life experience. As I got older, I started to defy all authoritative figures in my life, from my grandparents to my coaches. I became angry without knowing exactly why, but sports became my outlet to leave it all on the field. But it was a temporary fix; it never fixed the root of the issue. It simply helped a little for the time being.

After frequently bumping heads with my grandparents, I decided to give living with my mom a try. I moved in with her at 17 and that only lasted a year. If I had to choose between describing myself as a lover or a fighter, I would say I'm a lover who would stab someone if that's what was needed. My grandparents instilled in us the principle that walking away from conflict was the right thing to do, and for many years, I bought into that concept. So when this girl at school pushed me after finding out I kissed her boyfriend, I didn't retaliate. I never got out of character when it came to strangers. Oddly enough, I had only been in one fight and that was with my mom. But with my mom, it was just different. This was a woman who was supposed to love me but would often go out of her way to provoke me. One day, I snapped and picked up a kitchen knife, knowing I had no business even acting like I was going to do something with it. I was never scared of her - I just had enough of her bullying. I threw the knife and lunged for her. My eyes went black and my long-awaited fury possessed my physical body. I held onto her hair so tight that I could feel the acrylic on my nails lifting. I kept punching her until she got me in a chokehold. As soon as we separated, she threatened to do what many people would expect a white lady to say, that she was going to call the police. I fled immediately; what person of color wants to be face-to-face with a police officer when their mom is white? From the strength of pure adrenaline, I ran from our house all the way to the soccer fields where my team was practicing ten miles away. When I finally arrived, I told my coach what happened and called my grandparents to come save me from the white devil. My grandpa swooped in to rescue me like Shrek did Fiona in the tower from the fire-breathing dragon. The next day, I went to get my belongings from my mom's place and moved back in with my grandparents to finish my high school years. The thing that drove me nuts about my mom is how she would act like a complete lunatic one minute and then turn around and act as if nothing ever happened. She has always been a person to sweep everything under the rug, ignoring the Mount Olympus-sized pile of dust towering in the center of it. She was manipulative and would say whatever it took to make everything seem normal again - although nothing was ever normal in the first place.

Outside of the issues at home, I never had it easy with guys. The ones I liked always went for the girls who had bigger assets, wore makeup I couldn't afford, and were top of the food chain in terms of popularity. I always admired the beauty of these women, wishing I could be seen in the same light as them, but I was never green with envy. I just couldn't understand why I wasn't good enough to be noticed. What was wrong with me? I thought I was pretty, I wasn't the most popular, but throughout the years, I won the "Who's Who" awards for being a class favorite, athletic and friendliest. I did have very troublesome, acne-prone skin and didn't learn how to accurately apply makeup until later in my 20's. I straightened my hair every day to resemble all the other girls because I knew of no other beauty standard in my predominately-white school, and as a result, my hair suffered so much heat damage that I had to wear weave to feel pretty. A rough day of people making fun of the thickness of my eyebrows led me to go home and pluck off 90% of them. The next day, I got made fun of even worse. The lesson here was that you will never win with people.

My grandparents did the best they could to provide, but it's not like I came from money. We lived in an uppity area where kids were driving G-Wagons to school, yet I was pulling into the senior parking lot in a silver Dodge Caravan with a door that didn't open on one side. It was confusing to watch ditzy girls with D-cups and ditzy boys with D1 dreams being glorified. They had such a sense of entitlement without any actual substance.

I must admit, not having everything I wanted handed to me taught me valuable lessons. I knew of humility and formed strong social skills, unlike many of my counterparts who were born into money or society's standard of beautiful their entire lives. In the looks department, I didn't stand out, but I always treated everyone equally, the same way I'd want to be treated. It wasn't some forced sympathetic thought to be nice to kids from different cliques; it just came naturally to be kind. Even though I was a star athlete, I knew what it was like to feel invisible. You never know what a person is going through and how a simple "hi" in the hallway could make them feel like they matter. I know because I was one of those people. I never expected anything in return for being a decent human being, but it would make me smile when the people I spoke to made an effort to return the favor in passing.

Our soccer community made it possible for me to play travel ball by covering the majority of the club expenses. We couldn't afford it, but they came together knowing I needed the exposure. It took an entire village to ensure I got my ass to college. After completing my four years of high school, I prepared to make my collegiate debut that fall on a full soccer scholarship to a popular HBCU. I was excited but also very nervous to go from being one of the few token black girls on my team to attending an all-black college. I grew to a point of wanting to know and embrace my black side more after being deprived of it. I didn't even know I was mixed - or what it meant to be mixed - until late in middle school. Where others were concerned about my transition, I felt more ready than ever before. I was eager for a fresh start in a new place and to explore a side of myself that had been so foreign to me throughout my early life.

80 ✿ C03

SETH
Finding Oz

All the student-athletes were ordered to attend a mandatory meeting in the gym to get prepped and squared away for the fall semester. All the excess noise and chatter quieted the moment I laid my eyes upon you for the very first time. I admit that at that moment, I fell in love with the idea of you. There you stood, a seemingly perfect human, tall with tanned skin from the summer's sun and dark silky hair. I felt frozen in time, taking in this beautiful stranger with the striking smile. I was determined to get your attention, so I began to have an obnoxiously loud conversation about music with your teammate behind me. I was hoping you'd chime in - you didn't, but you acknowledged you overheard us. It was the first encounter of many more to come.

Seeing you around campus became the highlight of my day. I found myself scanning the crowds of people between classes and during lunch with the anticipation of finding you. We mainly saw one another in passing after practice, but you expressed no interest. You occasionally looked my way but I never held your gaze for long. What was a girl to do? Be satisfied with these silent exchanges that probably didn't mean a damn thing to you but were everything to me? Was I to wait around? Twiddle my thumbs? Pray for you until God grew weary of my begging? Make a wish whenever I saw 11:11? It had been weeks and still no word or initiation on your part. I was tired of waiting. Dogs chase pussy, men chase what they want, and I wasn't going to be the one chasing you. It was obvious the feelings weren't mutual, so my pride forced me to put an end to this far-fetched fantasy.

One night hanging out on the plaza, this green-eyed basketball player I had seen around campus approached me. I could feel everyone's eyes on us, trying to decipher what was to come of the situation. He was one of the most sought-after athletes at our school, and I had no fucking clue why, out of all the girls to pick from, he chose me. After a bit of generic small talk, we exchanged phone numbers. I was excited to find out more about him. I soon learned he was a terrible texter who abbreviated words like "what", "are" and "you," senselessly. His lack of urgency and brain cells didn't stop me from sneaking into his dorm room to have sex. It didn't take long for that fling to fizzle out after finding out he had a reputation of trying to talk to everybody. I was just another girl, another body, another hole for him to fuck.

This is the first time in years I have revisited these memories, Seth. They're still so vivid for me. I hate how much I adored you.

Your teammate was talking to my teammate, so they set it up for all of us to hang out. We walked over to your apartment off-campus for a night of fun since the dorms had so many unnecessary rules. Our personalities immediately showed their strength and opposition in conversation. "Like when a tornado meets a volcano," *isn't that right?* You were even more beautiful up close and personal. Your eyes were like everything Emerald City represented. You were so certain of all the bullshit that came out of your mouth. You would've made a fantastic lawyer or cult leader -both able to spin their moral corruption as righteous to benefit their selfish desires.

Once we all got settled in, you put on *Boondocks Saints* for us to watch. Must've been a good movie, seeing how you had a poster of it hanging up on your living room wall. I wouldn't know because not even five minutes into it, I left. I was completely caught off guard when you mentioned you had a girlfriend. My teammate didn't object to me leaving, but it left the boys confused as to how things escalated so quickly. All this time, all these hopes…wasted. Had I known you were in a relationship, I would have never agreed to tag along to your apartment in the first place. *Is anything in life worth having easy?*

My dramatic exit didn't stop you from asking your teammate to ask mine for my phone number. In fact, I think you were intrigued by the unexpected turn of events that night. When you make someone feel unimportant, there is a shift in power when the opposing party needs you to validate their ego. If you didn't care that you had a girlfriend at home, then why should I? Not my relationship, not my problem. Besides, this was college. *Why not have a little fun?*

The next week, I came to your apartment. I was alone. There was a tense energy that thickened the air between the two of us. It felt like a game of Air Hockey, each of us testing the other. You left the living room to use the bathroom in your bedroom. Once you closed the door behind you, I walked into your bedroom. You didn't have many things, but something on your dresser stood out, almost staring at me. It was a fully-clothed Build-A-Bear. You came out of the bathroom as I was holding it, and without hesitation, I asked about its significance. "My girlfriend, Jean, gave it to me," you said flatly. I looked at the bear in utter disgust, speechless. Who gives a grown man a stuffed animal? I'll tell you who - a naive, blindly loyal girl who thinks life is a romance novel, all while her less-than-dreamy boyfriend was spending his time with other women, that's who.

I didn't want to storm out; I knew what I originally walked back into. I felt like there was nothing to lose at this point, as my throat began to fill with word vomit. With the odds stacked against me, my confidence changed the momentum of our conversation. I started asking forward questions I would've never had the balls to ask if I wasn't so discouraged by the corny-ass sentimental teddy bear. You explained you had a girlfriend of five years who you loved dearly back home. You even showed me the pictures of her on your phone. I said she was pretty, but I lied. The chunky highlights in her hair were tacky, and even imagining her without the braces, she was average at best. She wasn't me. You were sure to inform me that you could've lied about your situation like all your teammates did, but you wanted to be honest with me. I should've left. I should've never been at your place. *Why was I here? What was making me stay?* It's funny how you were so in love yet found refuge in my guts later that night. Words mean nothing when the flesh is weak.

Did it bother me you had a girlfriend? *Absolutely.* Was I going to honor girl code and do the right thing? Absolutely *not*. As an athlete, I have always had a competitive spirit and this was no different. I played to win, and from the moment I saw you at the gym, I wanted you to be mine. If you want something bad enough, you'll do whatever it takes, *right*? We became inseparable. I didn't stay in my dorm room much after that and only went back to get more clothes. Poof! Before we realized what was happening, we were playing house. I loved doing simple things with you. You made life more exciting. One of our weekly rituals was grocery shopping and renting a movie from Red Box. I didn't even know how to boil water so you often cooked for us. I felt like we were in our own little world together, just the two of us.

As our connection deepened, it was no coincidence when you randomly asked me if I had slept with anyone at school. I blanked for what felt like a minute before actually answering. *I finally snag the man of my dreams and now all he's concerned about is who I've slept with before him?* I guess us being there in that moment wasn't enough. You wanted to hear that you were the only guy I did this with, to justify continuing a relationship with me. I knew if I had told you the truth, I'd lose everything I worked so desperately to gain. We were just starting out; the other athlete before you meant nothing to me. I felt ashamed knowing I fell short of the woman you wanted me to be, but I was determined to win you over. I've always been a bad liar, but that day, I gave my best Oscar-worthy performance. I could tell you knew I was lying, but you decided to believe me for the moment. It was frightening to know the magnitude of this lie when your demeanor immediately became relaxed.

Why did it matter to you so much? I came to college single, ready to mingle, unlike you. Experimenting was the norm, unlike your situation. What secure person questions someone about their past to only place judgment? It happened, people learn, why harp? A girl fucks two guys in two months and is suddenly not worth the time? Did I mention you still had a girlfriend? Or did you forget? I wasn't in a relationship with you, she was. I was free to do whatever I wanted, but I chose to be exclusive with you. My pussy was yours even when you'd go back home on holidays and share my dick. I didn't feel bad for long because my lie bought me more time with you. I just wanted to be good enough for someone like you, and I knew in time, you would see I was. If I only had a brain...

You and Jean took each other's virginity, so with my track record, I was at a disadvantage in terms of fitting the perfect girlfriend criteria. I was younger than you but had more bodies, which you would frequently remind me how bad that made me look. It was impossible to compete with Miss Goody Two Shoes and her untainted pussy. I was trashy yet she was the one being cheated on. Virgin Mary's box couldn't have been that divine if you couldn't resist mine. Besides, I was in a better position than her and that was my edge. You were lying to her every night to lay up with me.

I never thought I would be someone's, other woman. I knew I was better than being the side-chick, but I was too enamored with the possibilities of what my life could be with you. In my heart, I didn't think you wanted to cheat either; you were just unhappy in your relationship but didn't quite know how to get out of it. I should've won an award for Side Piece of the Century for all the little things I did. When Jean called, I would quietly leave the room. Sometimes I would kiss you on your neck to distract you from whatever she was blabbing about. I loved that I could make you smile.

Jean came down to visit on one of her school breaks. Prior to her arrival, you told me I wouldn't be hearing from you since you'd be spending time with her. I stayed in my dorm room those few days while you shared our bed with that bitch. My roommate asked me what was going on because my being there was a rarity, so I told her. After I explained what was transpiring, she suggested that I cut you off completely or text your phone in hopes that Jean would see. Neither of those ideas crossed my mind; the thought of losing you made me sick to my stomach. I had no loyalty to Jean; she was the enemy! She had what I wanted, and if she thought I would leave your life without a fight, she was sadly mistaken. I was on the Yellow Brick Road, headed to war for you. I was patient, and besides, she was going back home soon.

Over what felt like the slowest days known to mankind, I grew angrier with each hour I had to spend in my dorm away from your love. I hated not talking to you. Why was I being so cooperative? Why was I playing my role so well? How did I get here? The pain became too much to bear and I needed to let it out somehow. My roommate had left for a tournament that weekend, so I had our humble abode all to myself. From our window, I could see the dorm where your teammates stayed and you often visited. You always parked in the same spot, so I was periodically checking to see your car. I had a cross necklace I occasionally wore when I felt temporarily "wholesome." I walked over to my desk in tears, found the necklace, and removed the pendant. I got my straightener out from under my desk and turned it on. I was sitting down in my chair as I caught a glimpse of my reflection in my vanity mirror. I hated how you made me feel. I placed the pendant on my straightener to heat up for a few minutes and pressed the cross into my flesh. The burning pain was such a relief to me; I knew I deserved to hurt. I got myself into this and I needed to be punished. I lost count of the number of times I repeated this but by the time I was finished, my skin had welted. The burning sensation didn't distract from the overwhelming sadness that lingered over my heart.

I was hurting, Seth. You hurt me. After all the time we spent together, countless laughs, and in-depth conversations, it all meant nothing to you when you were with her. You were a pitiful excuse for a man with your corrupted double life. When my roommate returned, she immediately noticed my self-inflicted burn. She tried to reason with me, saying there wasn't any man alive worth this agony, but who the fuck was she? She didn't know you like I did! I didn't want to argue, so I simply wiped my eyes and thanked her for her advice. I even entertained the thought of leaving you alone like it was an actual option. It wasn't; you were mine and I was determined to have you forever. I think this was the moment I knew I was in love with you.

Seven months in and you tell me you want to be faithful to your girlfriend? Is this real life? You're joking, right? Just like that?

Everything was just fine the day before, and then you hit me randomly with this? No warning signs - just a text breaking off everything we worked so hard to build. A text, *really*? You didn't even have the decency to tell me face-to-face. Of course, you did it through text because you and I both knew that was the only way you could carry out that promise. We were officially done. I felt my heart break into microscopic pieces and fall into the pit of my stomach. I thought what we had was special, but you proved the feelings were far from mutual.

I can't tell you how many times I cried. I was miserable without you; it felt like a piece of me was missing. My pride refused to let you see how much being apart from you killed me inside. A couple weeks later, I had a dinner date lined up for Valentine's Day with a super shy - but totally hot - baseball player. I wasn't the slightest bit interested in him, but he was cute enough to pass the time. He had the warmest smile, but he wasn't you. I figured everyone was going to keep falling short in comparison if I didn't at least make an attempt to move on with my life. Doesn't it suck when you have to break up with someone you never technically dated? Even though you weren't near, our hearts were still in sync. You knew I was moving on. If I knew you like I knew I knew you, you were losing your mind at the thought of me with someone else. I couldn't stop thinking about you. I never stopped loving you. During our time apart, I didn't sleep with anyone. I missed your touch too much to allow another to touch me. How I longed to hear your voice, to look into your eyes, to be on top of you again. My heart belonged to you.

Not talking to you only lasted a few weeks. We could never

resist each other. You pitched a tent in my head and camped out, cooking my heart like s'mores on the open fire. We were so bad for one another but everything felt so fucking good. You came back with a bang and gave me some of the most unforgettable birthday sex of my life. People who say angry sex is the best sex have never had "I miss you" sex. I experienced my first orgasm with you. You don't realize what you've been missing until you've had your first orgasm. If you aren't sure if you've had an orgasm or not, then most likely, you haven't. You would know because your vagina explodes with euphoria.

Being back in your arms felt like home. The first time you attempted to tell me you loved me, we were in the Walmart parking lot. You said you were in love with Jean, but you loved me. I didn't know what that meant exactly; I simply heard you mention me and love in the same sentence. I was disappointed you didn't just come out and say it, but I was happy that you gave me some iota of hope. I loved you long before you were able to admit it out loud that you were falling for me. I wanted you to be mine for the rest of my life.

As much time I had already invested, I grew tired of waiting for you to leave her. Whenever I brought it up, you'd dismiss it and say it wasn't that simple. You weren't happy, and I made you happy, so you should be with me. You were prolonging the inevitable and only making it harder for when the time was to come. You didn't love your girlfriend that much because I was still in the picture, almost a year later. I knew the truth, she didn't, and if the truth is an act of love, who did you really love? I always wondered how you were able to live a double life so effortlessly. All the juggling of conversations, emotions, names, memories - did you ever get tired of waking up and lying? Liars rarely do, why do the right thing when you can have it your way, huh? What a life. You had the luxury of two women who were willing to do whatever it took to keep you around, even if it meant having no respect for themselves. Seems pretty pathetic, but nothing short of ideal to the average narcissist.

Jean called you on a summer afternoon; she found out about us. Well, she could finally prove she knew about me, about us, and your double life. She had checked your bank statements and saw some purchases that would have stood out to anyone. You'd bought a few items from Victoria's Secret that she never received because they weren't for her - they were for me. After you got off the phone with her, you called me to break the news.

Despite all the evidence presented, Jean pleaded that you two had too much history to "throw away over a college fling." Little did she know, I was much more than a fling. You see, when you're on the side, you get a bird's-eye view of what the "main" partner is not doing. A bench player wants what most starters take for granted - the opportunity to play. "Hard work beats talent when talent doesn't work hard." If you're not excited to suck your man's dick when he walks through the door sweaty, there's someone who will be honored to do it. It's not fair, but sometimes that someone just so happens to be on the sideline warming up to sub you out.

She was willing to overlook everything if you were able to confess you enjoyed sex with her more. You loved fucking me; you couldn't get enough of me. Whenever you wanted it, however you wanted it, your wish was my command. There was never a time I didn't want you inside me. My wetness gave me away, making it an easy slide for home. Do you remember that? I didn't even know how to ride, but each time I got back on the horse with the saddle strapped. I was overjoyed you told her the truth by saying you didn't. This was the breakthrough I had been waiting for! Ten months later, and you were officially single. All of my teammates, family, and friends said you would never in a million years leave her for me, but you did. You went against everything in your comfort zone for a chance at happiness with little ol' me. I couldn't contain my excitement as I drove back home to share the news. My grandma never liked you. She always questioned how good of a guy could you be if you did such a thing to your girlfriend of five years. To me, her opinion stemmed from an outdated place, so I didn't give it much thought. I never wanted to hear anything negative that anyone - including my grandma - had to say about you. My efforts and tears had finally paid off. You were soon to be all mine.

We spent the majority of the summer together because I'd drive up to see you while you were taking summer courses. One weekend, you surprised me by driving down to visit me at my mom's. My grandma wasn't here for our union so I temporarily made nice with my mom in order for us to be able to see one another. I heard a knock at the door, and as I slowly opened it, I saw that infectious smile spread across your face. I couldn't believe you drove down just to see me. No time with you ever felt long enough. That night, we had sex eight times. We were so lost in one another; it was just the two of us in our own little world. I felt like I could look into your eyes until the end of time. I always thought I was the lucky one to have you. There was a part of me that needed you to make me feel whole. You were my everything. You filled the gaping holes in my heart.

It was finally just the two of us, but the problems with Jean had merely begun. You were her first everything; she knew no life without your guidance. You had trouble with the law a while back, and even at your lowest, she was by your side. That didn't stop you from treating her as if it all meant nothing. Being a woman, I was able to empathize with how painful this must have been for her, but I can't say I ever felt any guilt. Boohoo, poor Jean. She knew about us the entire time and made the choice to tolerate your bullshit. It was her decision to not see the truth for what it was. Unfortunately, that didn't stop her from blowing up your phone. I suppose that's what you do when you really love someone or had she no dignity?

She called you one day crying about how she had sex with some guy, and she didn't want to be with anyone else but you. With that confession, she put the final nail in her own coffin for any potential relationship there could have been between the two of you. Her uncharted pooty was the one thing she always had over me. Now that she had nothing more to leverage, you saw her as a filthy whore who was able to fuck someone else fresh off a breakup. Jean played so devastated, yet wasted no time hopping to the next dick. You told me how you admired the fact that yours was the only dick I let penetrate me, even when our future seemed unknown. I understood why she did it, but all is fair in love and war. I was happy to know you were seeing her for the dumb bitch she truly was. I never saw your attitude towards Jean as problematic because you treated us differently. Things were going to be different with us, or so at least I thought.

It was a couple months post-breakup, and the mad cow was still calling and texting your phone. One morning, a three-part text from Jean woke me up out of my sleep. I looked over and there you still laid, sound asleep. I glanced at the time and saw it was too fucking early to be this pitiful. Why couldn't she just let it go? Why was she stuck on someone that didn't want her? That didn't respect her? There was nothing she could do to get you back at this point. You belonged to me because I earned your love. History holds no torch to a person who makes you happier. I was furious! I woke you up out of your sleep and told you this had to stop; it was now disturbing my peace. Instead of ignoring her like you typically would, I told you to set her straight once and for all. You were willing to do anything to make me happy, so you told her to stop bothering you and move on. After all, you left her to be with me.

You asked me to officially be your girlfriend, and the next day, you got a call from your mom about how Jean tried to kill herself. You placed the blame on me since I was the one who told you to make her leave you alone. She tried to overdose on Tylenol PM, but when she realized what she had done, she had her friend call 911. She was rushed to the hospital where she had her stomach pumped. I felt horrible, but we hadn't even been a couple a full 24 hours, and this shit happened. I don't think suicide is a laughing matter; I was just too fucking angry to sympathize outside of my own selfishness. I raged with jealousy while you cried in my arms. I thought your tears were an indication of you wanting her back, and I couldn't let that happen. I should have been more present for you emotionally, but I couldn't. The thought of losing you again was too much for me to bear.

Is this too honest for you? You've already read this far; do you really think I'm going to sugarcoat the shit now? Yeah, it's a touchy subject - I get it - but this is my truth. There is much to unravel, so stay focused.

We got into an argument over my cold demeanor and short responses. According to you, I wasn't mature enough to enter this ring, I was in search of something no man could compensate for. Later that night, for the first time, you told me you loved me. Our bond was sickening; we both were ill, but our love was the cure. As much as I despised that cunt, I prayed for her as much as I didn't want to because I wasn't some totally heartless bitch. I was just in love with you.

As the fall semester came to an end, there was no separating us. I was never really seen around campus once we became more serious. I missed a lot of school functions because they seemed to be a recipe for disaster to any monogamous relationship. What was I looking for at parties that I didn't already have? I regret not taking in more of the rich culture our school had to offer, such as celebrating events like Homecoming or the Halloween parties, but I was in love. On a campus of 10,000, all I saw was you. I decided to leave school, soccer, and everything I knew to move to Indiana with you. I had no idea how I would make money, what my family would think, or what I even wanted to do with my life, but I didn't care. As long as I had you, you would be all I needed. My grades were already on the decline due to my lack of focus, so I figured, *why the hell not run off with the love of my life?* In our world, we had no rules - just love. I couldn't find a fuck to give if it didn't pertain to you.

You reassured me I didn't have to leave. You said we could make the long-distance thing work, but I knew when you were lying. I already had my mind made up. I didn't need friends because *you* were my friend. I didn't need a family because *you* were my family. You were my everything, and I refused to live a life without you in it. Even when I entertained the idea of staying, you became passive-aggressive about my indecisiveness. I was looking for the smallest ounce of support from you - almost permission - to be able to leave it all behind. Once you gave me the green light, we were all packed up on the road, ready to embark on a new chapter together. Nothing about our story was traditional or anything you'd see on the Hallmark Channel. It was wrong in every sense of the word, and rather demented. Soccer was my first love, but I replaced it with you. I walked away from a full scholarship and a team that I grew to love to be with you. From varsity to a travel team, to Division I, to a short-lived semi-professional career, I had achieved more than I ever wanted. The accolades and championships seemed minuscule in the grand scheme of loving you.

I scrapped everything I knew and thought I wanted for myself in exchange for the possibilities of our life together. My aunt told me not to lose myself in any man and to have something of my own, but it was a little late for that. If I could do it all over again, I would do nothing differently. I always knew meeting you would change my life. I never understood why at the time, but from the moment I saw you, it was a feeling that never left me. Regret weighs much more than trying, so I didn't hesitate to follow my heart.

After traveling almost a thousand miles to our new home, we finally made it. Well, not our new home, but instead the basement in your parents' home. The house itself was fairly old, but with you, it felt like an underground palace. I didn't like your family from the day I met them. You guys had all these inside jokes you'd drag on that were never funny. Surprisingly, they never got any funnier, no matter how many times they were retold. I was just mad I was never included and felt like an outsider. I often reminded myself that graduating from side chick and promoted to a girlfriend serious enough to meet the family was a huge deal. I forgot where I came from and was quickly humbled to even be in their presence. I was going to make the best of the situation, even if it meant faking it until I made it.

I have always been sensitive, especially to energy. Maybe it's just a Pisces thing or an overall woman thing, but I knew from day one that your Mom didn't like me. I always caught her sizing me up and acting like I wasn't in the same room when she was talking to you. She didn't like the way you transitioned from Jean to me so quickly and without warning. Your brother's girlfriend told me your mom said she liked Jean better than me, which made bonding even harder to do when I knew her true feelings. I became obsessed with the thought of finding proof for my theory. As I strategically gained your mom's trust, I learned her Facebook password from when she needed help resetting it. I logged into her account the next day when she left for work that morning. To no surprise, I saw that she was still communicating with Jean about missing her and even brought me up to a few of her friends. That old bitch! Had she no loyalty? I knew you were unaware of this and wasted no time to tell you of my findings. It wasn't the brightest decision, because my emotions caused me to incriminate myself as a hacker, but it was worth it. You confronted her without telling her how you obtained the information because you always took my side.

The first Christmas at your family's house was a nightmare I couldn't wake up from. One of your brothers accidentally called me by Jean's name when asking me to pass the present closest to me. It didn't take long for me to excuse myself to the bathroom since I couldn't hold back the tears a second longer. This was more challenging than I anticipated. Why was Jean so hard for everyone to erase? You had moved onto someone better - me! Right after I closed the bathroom door, I sank to the floor. I threw myself a private pity party - a party of one - all types of fun. Crying didn't make the pain go away instantly, but it sure made me feel better in the moment. I realized if I didn't find a way to pull it together, I'd be in the bathroom all of Christmas Day. Slowly, I began to wipe my tears away, reminding myself what I signed up for. I don't know if I was more disappointed your brother couldn't differentiate names or how long it took you to finally check on me. I knew Jean would've gotten the sickest pleasure from knowing that her presence was very much still alive. I had to tell myself, *I'm here now, not her.* I took a deep breath and put on my best-strained smile.

After the holidays, you left to go to train for the draft. I was alone to fend for myself. My new life was miserable. I had no family. None of your friends' girlfriends wanted to be my friend because of their loyalty to Jean, and I was having difficulty keeping a job. Your dad stepped in and helped me land a first-shift factory gig at his workplace. I struggled to make it to work, considering it was still dark outside when it was supposed to be morning. That fiasco only lasted two weeks; any longer and I would've taken a blowtorch to my neck to sever my head. I tried AT&T Cable door-to-door sales in a shirt my boss gave me "new" yet it reeked of B.O. I was even a server at my favorite Italian restaurant in town, but unfortunately, I didn't like working there as much as I did eating their food. After the list of odd jobs with unsuccessful outcomes grew longer, I eventually got hired at a nightclub downtown. I made a few friends I shared no real similarities with other than where we worked, but I was thankful for some human interaction. You were away chasing your dreams while I scrambled to find passion. I would often go home, eat, and hide out in the basement to avoid forced conversations with your family upstairs. I found the most comfort in isolation. I thought this was going to be different; I thought we were in this together. I thought this was going to just be the two of us.

Jean still hadn't let you go. She was constantly running her mouth on social media for everyone to see. I knew my retaliation would've given her the validation she was so desperately seeking. She wanted to matter to you by mattering to me. My pride was too strong to show how much it hurt my feelings. I couldn't let anyone – particularly her - see me sweat, even if I was drenched in it. She was your ex-girlfriend - of course, I was creeping on her page. I wasn't intimidated by her; I was more annoyed by her audacious arrogance. Little did she know, I knew where she worked, the hours she was bartending, what her car looked like, and the location of her parents' house she lived in across the street from Planned Parenthood. Whenever I'd go to the gym or run errands, I would drive by to see if she was home, and if she was home, I wondered what she was doing. All of that shit-talking online, I could've easily slashed her tires. Better yet, I could've set her family's house on fire. One minute, they're dreaming of it raining gumdrops, and the next, they're engulfed in flames screaming bloody murder, all thanks to their wretched daughter. It's important to be mindful of the things you say to others because you just never know what type of person is on the receiving end. I spared her time after time again, and you fucking knew it. I talked to you about it, but you dismissed the whole ordeal as childish on both ends. "She would never fight; she's not like that," you said. You just told me to quit stalking but had you put her in her place, to begin with, we wouldn't be here! If you didn't care about it, it didn't matter how it made anyone else feel. Your world of selfish oblivion held no place for me. I dropped the discussion and decided to still keep an eye on her quietly.

One weekend, I was randomly assigned to work the door to

collect admission for the nightclub. As the line started moving, I spotted some familiar faces waiting in it. It was Jean, and she had brought a couple friends with her. This was my first time seeing Jean in person since we were dating. I could hear my heartbeat in my throat as it raced with adrenaline wondering how I was going to handle a situation that had been so troublesome in my personal life. All I could think about was the constant harassment and evil words she carelessly spewed online about me when she didn't even know me. This was my moment - I was finally going to be face-to-face with the girl who hated my guts for taking her boyfriend. Once it was their turn to pay for admission, I was looking directly at the person the man I loved used to love. She didn't make any eye contact with me but I never took my eyes off her. I wasn't surprised at how basic she looked in person. I'm not sure why I expected more.

I couldn't wrap my mind around the fact that at one point, she made you happy for so long. As she and her friends approached the entrance, I thought about all of the wildly uncool and terrible things I could say or do to her. I was extremely unprepared for this series of events. I didn't have a game plan for how I wanted to portray my demeanor after months of torment. *Should I act like I didn't know who they were? Say a snide remark? Giggle facetiously? Whisper to security that I read on Facebook they're here to cause trouble? Or lose my job to punch her square in the face?* There were so many options but I had to think fast on my feet as I was running out of time. Jean's tall friend had added me on Facebook not too long before, so I recognized her face. She actually said hi to me, which stunned me. I

37

still couldn't believe Jean didn't look up once. What's the matter, hun? Cat got your tongue?

As she and her friends started to pull out their money, I interrupted them by saying "You guys are good." *Really, Brittany? You just let them in for free?!* I couldn't believe it my damn self! Maybe in the back of my mind, I knew that if I were her, I would feel the same way. For a second, I almost felt bad for what I did. Girls fighting over a guy seemed like such a disservice to the strong women before us who banded together fighting for equality. Unfortunately, this wasn't just any guy and we can't all win in love's battlefield.

My feelings of remorse were short-lived. After our run-in, the little twat took to Twitter to call me a "broke bitch" and a "butterface." I was struggling financially and couldn't afford to keep my phone on consistently, but how did she know that? Either way, I was impressed because she had done her research on me as well. I don't know how I expected her to react but she really had no room for the name-calling. I could've commented about her evident post-breakup weight gain, but my golden heart wouldn't allow me to hit that far below the belt.

HALFWAY POINT

Halfway through your chapter, Seth, and the best is yet to come. Do you ever look back at our relationship and wonder why you said and did all this shit to me? Do you see the error in the way you treated me? Do you hold yourself accountable for anything? Or was everything my fault? Do you try to break your fiancée down like you did me? Probably not, because let you tell it, our undoing was my fault. I really fucking loved you.

I can't name one thing I didn't do to keep you happy. I would've moved mountains for you if you wanted them out of the way. By the way you acted towards me, you'd think I was you and you were me. You made me feel so alone in our relationship. You never complimented me much; it's not like I needed the constant reassurance, but it would've been nice to hear you say I looked pretty. I put so much time and effort into getting ready just for you to say nothing. I would always tell you when you looked nice, even though in my eyes, I thought that was all the time. Even when you'd gripe about needing a haircut or to shave, in my mind, you looked perfect. Maybe I was asking for too much. We had been together for a couple years already, so since we were past the cupcake phase, my expectations were unrealistic. I was your girlfriend; that fact alone should've weighed more than the desire for any measly compliment. Maybe I was too needy. Maybe I just wanted the person I was in love with to act like he loved me back.

It always seemed like couples were fighting over cheating. I didn't want you to ever feel like you needed to cheat on me. I wanted to be everything you had ever dreamed of and more. My logic was that if we removed the cheating dynamic, what would there be left to argue about? Threesomes…that's it! What if we had threesomes together? One of our favorite rap artists Joe Budden and his girlfriend did it and displayed it for the world to see on national television. They seemed happy, so why not us?

I was the cool girlfriend that could tag along on guys' nights and on all the spontaneous trips to places where men went to cheat like Las Vegas. I never acted jealous or sensitive, so I was awarded privileges your friend's girlfriends weren't granted. They had to stay at home while I got to see how men really operate when they're away from their women. I just wanted you to be proud to call me your girl. All of your friends always told you how lucky you were to have someone like me. Too bad you didn't feel that way.

Tensions grew between your mom and me, so we temporarily moved to Ohio to stay with my aunt. We spent a lot of nights centimeters apart on the couch, searching Instagram for our first girl. We even went as far as to join dating sites to see what they had to offer. I never spoke to any potential girl directly; when they thought they were talking to me, they were really communicating back and forth with you. It was always you posing as me. You took nudes of me so we could get theirs in return. You treated me like an object; there was no personal attachment. You were nurturing a piglet for slaughter. I thought these things were strengthening our bond since nobody else could relate to us. I thought what we had was special.

Our first threesome was with one of my co-workers at Victoria's Secret. Her name was Lila. She was younger than me, not the brightest, but cute nonetheless. Aunt Cindy went on a cruise with her girls for a few days, so she left us in charge of her three dogs. We had the whole place to ourselves! Everything aligned perfectly, and I knew it was no coincidence. I invited Lila over that night, but since the dogs weren't fond of the mysterious company, all three of us went down into the basement with a full bottle of Southern Comfort.

After a few shots later, it just happened. There was a brief pause after senseless subject-hopping before she and I started kissing. I never knew what kissing a woman would feel like, but there was no difference other than it feeling like a necessary evil. A minute or so later, we stopped laughing off the nervousness of what just happened between seemingly innocent co-workers. How did we get here? Before we knew it, the bottle was down to its last drop. One minute, we're all smiles. The next minute, Lila was barfing. She threw up all over my aunt's brand new white carpet she just raved about getting installed. I have never sobered up so quickly in my entire life because even those shots couldn't numb the realization that my aunt was going to fucking kill me when she saw what we had done.

I freaked out, killing whatever was left of my buzz since this dumb heaux decided to conveniently vomit in the middle of the floor. I was coherent enough to tell you to grab the carpet cleaner from the laundry room. Even you who had a much higher tolerance for alcohol, you stood no match for the Southern Comfort either. As soon as you started spraying the carpet, I noticed something peculiar about the bottle…it was BLEACH! I looked down to see the snow-white carpet turning orange right before my very eyes. I was too tipsy to care, but I was crying on the inside. The puke stain had dried to what resembled a penis - the irony. Not only did we bleach my Aunt's new carpet, but we left a dick print as a landmark of this moment.

The three of us relocated upstairs to escape the mess and made our way to the bedroom. I don't think there was anything I could've done to prepare myself mentally for what was about to happen. The time had come. Our first threesome began to unfold after Lila and I began making out in a similar fashion as we did in the basement. Clothes started coming off and hands were touching everything in close proximity. It was happening people! She was on top of me kissing me while you fucked her. We switched places for a while, but you barely fucked me. At one point, you and Lila were so into one another that I started to question my reason for being there. She was moaning your name while you looked her in the eyes, stroking her in the missionary position. This was not what I imagined would happen. For a second, I could've sworn you enjoyed her pussy more than mine. Did you? Was I not enough? I was sitting at the edge of the bed, not knowing if I should attempt to participate or stay out of the way. I couldn't wait for it all to come to an end. Literally. You always came fairly quick, so my suffering didn't last too long. Why didn't you make me feel more included?

As soon as we finished - or should I say, *you and Lila* finished - I went downstairs to get some water. By "get some water," I mean that I really needed space to cry in peace. I felt angry, confused, and hurt, all in a matter of ten minutes. Can you imagine what it feels like witnessing the person you love fuck someone else? Watching them look the other person in the eyes like they do you? Watching them care enough to take their time with each stroke like they once did with you? Have you ever seen your man give the dick that was supposed to be yours so effortlessly to someone else? You came downstairs shortly after because you knew. I tried to explain how you made me feel, but you just blamed my feelings on my own insecurities. You said if I was so bothered, then why did I start it up with her in the basement, as if kissing wasn't a two-way street. I don't know, *maybe because I wanted to make you happy?* We got into a huge, quiet argument, like two parents trying not to wake a baby. Instead of resolving anything, you left me in the living room and went back upstairs. Leaving me alone to deal with our problems was something you began to master well.

I had a lot to take in. After sitting by myself thinking of what had just transpired, I began to see how this was, in fact, my fault. I mean, we did agree to it - you didn't hold a gun to my head. I wanted to do it. I thought I did at least. Was I being insecure? I did feel like she was prettier than me, but beauty is subjective. Was that the real reason behind my behavior? I found the courage to return upstairs after almost an hour. I peered into the bedroom and saw you two a reasonably good distance apart, so maybe it wasn't as deep as I was making it. I climbed in the middle where there was enough space for me, but you didn't budge. I knew you weren't really sleeping, I wasn't downstairs sulking for that long. I started to cuddle you, attempting to throw the white flag to show you I was truly sorry. I just wanted you to love me again. I ruined our first experience so I had to make things right. I started rubbing on you and slowly felt your body ease up. Before I knew it, we were at it again and Lila joined back in.

This time, I was the one to make you cum, so that made me feel more optimistic about everything. The next day, you told me despite my attempts to make the situation better, I failed miserably. You said you were so turned off by me that you didn't see me the same. You ended it by assuring me you would no longer be bringing threesomes up, and if I wanted to make it right, I would have to set the threesomes up on my own, proving I wasn't insecure. Needless to say, we had plenty more threesomes because I was determined to gain your trust back in me. Each time was different; it always felt unnatural and meaningless. We even went as far as to have a foursome with Lila and another co-worker of mine. The common denominator for all of these encounters were the guaranteed arguments afterward; they progressively began to worsen.

The women we hooked up with became escapes for my emptiness. They were always seeking affection when we finished, craving the closeness they were missing. They were never in a rush, like you, it was more about the journey for these women. I was confused about sexuality. I can specifically remember two girls that brought me to orgasm, and at that moment, I knew I was in deeper than I had ever anticipated. Percentage-wise, I know it's unlikely for women to orgasm from sex, but you didn't even try. Once you would finish, the girl and I always tended to cuddle like we were the ones in a relationship who brought *you* in and fucked *you*.

I made the interesting discovery that you didn't like the girls who were more into women. Everything was always about you, and for a woman not to be enamored by your greatness made her "lost" or lesser than the ones who were. You didn't like the girl we brought with us during Spring Break in Panama City Beach because she was more into the thought of me. When it was time to get it poppin', you were the first one to cum, but instead of stopping, she and I kept going. To show how unequal your views were, this pissed you off so much that you stormed out of the hotel room. Initially, I felt I should chase after you and make things right like I always did, but I didn't. This was the first time I discovered scissoring. I saw this when I'd flick the bean to lesbian porno flicks but never thought I'd ever get to try it. I got the hang of it once I caught a rhythm. When it came to hooking up with women, they always looked for me to fill the dominant role, so I couldn't appear like I didn't know what I was doing even when I didn't. As we went at it, this bitch said mid-stroke to tell her I loved her. For a moment, I almost broke complete focus, but I was too close to cumming to think about how bizarre the request really was. I thought, *if she's a bird, I'm a bird.* It caught me off guard, but I still told her I loved her and came right after. Are you surprised? I'm a simp with savage tendencies, but I said what I said to catch my nut. You and I ditched her once we got to the beach later that day and never spoke to her again. I should've felt bad about leaving her out to dry like that when I told her I loved her, but it's not like I meant it. Those phenomenal tits had me ready to say anything at the moment.

Sex with you began to feel like a chore - not for me, but for you. You didn't care as much and it would show. You never ate me out, let alone cared about my needs in general. You began going through the same series of positions, cum within minutes, throw me a towel, and head upstairs. How long did you expect this to continue, you not pleasing me? On top of our ritualistic sex life, we rarely cuddled post-sex. There was no intimacy after the intimacy.

I so desperately wanted you to be the one to bring me to climax, but you never did. Whenever I got close but it didn't happen right when you wanted it to, you threw your hands up in frustration. You lacked the patience to want to learn. These moments served as simple reminders that our whole relationship revolved around you. As our sex remained predictable and stagnant, I implemented an additional step after you threw me the towel and went upstairs. When the coast was clear and I heard the basement door close, I would masturbate.

I never watched porn or touched myself until my early 20's. When you were away overseas, I learned the sequence to ignite every inch of my body. It became a necessary habit to escape my dreary reality. I enjoyed porn at first, but I got bored watching the lack of real chemistry, over-the-top moaning, and bizarre phrases like "fuck that little hole." I graduated to something more realistic; I started to imagine what other men would be like. I thought about the way they would feel, how they smelled, the expression on their faces when they were about to cum, but most importantly, how they would've treated me. I wondered how they would be if put in your position.

Remember when I deleted my social media accounts for a year to prove my loyalty to you? Or how about when I had to ask for your approval to join an app called Instagram? When I originally joined Instagram, it served no real purpose other than posting pictures of my workouts and body. As my popularity grew, the further we grew apart. Since the pictures were rather risqué for the average audience, you insisted on keeping my page private and accepting females only. It got to a point where the number of requests kept making the app crash, so I eventually opened my page to the public. On the days when you'd play video games, I was in the basement with the iPad on our dresser thirst trappin before thirst trappin was thirst trappin to create a way out. You never gave me much attention, so taking pictures gave me something to look forward to and occupy my time.

One hundred thousand followers later, I was asked to do a video for Worldstar Hip Hop. I knew if I had any chance for the world to know my name, this was it. I was just a girl from Mississippi with a few thousand Instagram followers, and suddenly I was on a plane to Miami for a video shoot! A few months after my video debuted, I got my first paid club hosting. I couldn't believe I was being compensated to party when I had to work so hard at jobs I hated just to barely cover my bills. You were my manager, you negotiated all my emails, and

47

you even scheduled my first photoshoot with one of my favorite photographers I still use today, Jessy J. You were always pushing me to the point of tears because you saw my potential. It didn't make you any nicer; it just gave you more to take credit for and build your own ego. Once we got the ball rolling, there was no separating business and us. Sometimes, I just wanted to lay in the bed watching movies and eating popcorn with you, but you always kept us busy. Whether you heckled me about going to the gym or had me running routes for you in the front yard, it was nonstop. You were quick to talk about ideas to make money but never made time to talk about us. You never once asked me how I was feeling or what I wanted to do. Even when it wasn't about you, it was about you.

As unhappy as I was, I never once cheated on you. I never even so much as looked up when other guys were around. Some people will never cheat no matter how bad it is, just how some people will cheat no matter how good it is. You did a fantastic job constantly making me feel small and insignificant; I'm surprised I never stepped out on you. I was willing to chase you to the end of the Earth to get you to love me, but all that running began to wear and tear on my body. My legs were shaking with each step, hoping you'd turn around and carry me to the finish line. I crawled to your throne with my bloody heart in hand, begging for your mercy. You expecting me to combat all the outside attention with your mistreatment was like bringing a twig to a swordfight. I was holding out for the day you would finally wake up and just appreciate me. For a person who claimed to be the only guy to ever truly care about me, you sure made me feel disposable, like a cum rag. People I never thought would ever know I existed reached out to me in DM, and despite never entertaining them, it felt good to feel desired. What could they see that you couldn't?

You wanted to control every aspect of my life and I allowed you to do it. We spent the majority of the holidays with your family because you didn't really like mine. You had something negative to say about each of them and was extremely vocal about it to the point of embarrassment. Nobody in my family was married besides my grandparents, and each of us were too young in age to be popping out kids at the time. You took any opportunity to reinforce why your family was better and more together than mine. Yeah, your parents were married, but your dad had cheated on your mom and constantly talked down to her. He went out most nights only to come home reeking of beer from the local bar. Your mom's coping mechanism was a glass of wine and her precious Ambien. She would get real loose-lipped on those nights, but that was the only time I ever heard her say what she really felt. She shared a lot of things I had no business knowing, but I listened. None of your family acted like she existed, and since I was the only other female in the house going through something similar, we were able to relate.

Do you know how many people would have done anything to have a mom like yours? Here I am, at odds with my parents because they chose not to raise us, while you and your brothers took for granted the only thing I've ever wanted - a traditional household with both parents. Your dad's jokes about your mom's intelligence were idiotic and unamusing. I see where you got the characteristics of being an ass. Did you know you mimicked his behaviors? Parents are our first teachers, you know. If your own father didn't have respect for your mother, how could I expect you to have respect for me? You mirrored more than you realized, and your family was far from the Cleavers.

My family has never been perfect, but unlike you, I never claimed them to be so. I was primarily raised by my grandparents. That alone was abnormal. The only reason we had new clothes for school each year was because of my Aunt Cindy. My dad was equivalent to a stranger. My mom showed up on Christmas empty-handed every year but would buy things for the latest and greatest boytoy she was with for that week. I never wanted big expensive gifts, but if it's the same date every year, she could've at least saved up for a card. It was easy to look at my family in comparison to yours and find faults, but wasn't that normal? What was normal? What family has it all together? I let you convince me that mine wasn't good enough.

Out of everyone, my grandma worried about me the most, but I would rarely call. I was ready to cut off everyone and forget about them and be with you. If you didn't like them, I didn't either. I even ignored my two best friends from middle school Sherikka and Trahrissa because their opinions about you were too negative and too strong. I chose you over every person in my life because I felt like I didn't have much of a choice unless I wanted to visit home without you. Why did their opinions matter? I thought you treated me good enough; it was you and me against the world. Once I got rid of all the

50

emotional support I had in my corner, I found myself completely reliant on you.

You were determined to make me into your idea of the perfect woman. The whole reason I got into fitness was because of you. You were my muse, and I was your sponge. You had us on a strict diet and weight-gaining supplements because we both had a hard time keeping the pounds on. Naturally, I was fairly petite, so once I was religiously in the gym four times a week, I cut down to 125lbs of sheer muscle. You'd always tell me my body would be perfect if... "if" - is the key word here - I put on an extra 10lbs and got my boobs done. The more shakes I drank, the more ripped I became. I was so lean that the boobs I did develop from taking birth control vanished. You often made remarks about my muscular body shape, how I had no hips and saggy gorilla tits. You thought I forgot about you saying that when I was changing in the basement? You even went as far as to pull up a picture of a gorilla on Google images to show the accuracy of your comparison. I laughed with you to prevent myself from crying and starting an argument. If I only had the heart to admit I deserved better...

I felt so insecure about my body in the pursuit of seeking validation from you. You told me one of the best surgeons for breast augmentation was located in our city and suggested I look into it. You were so adamant about it that I started to believe I really could have the ideal figure if I just got them done. They were just boobs, right? After I thought long and hard about going under the knife, I couldn't bring myself to want to do it. I grew angrier each day at the thought of you trying to change me to fit your ideals. Nothing was wrong with my body, and I couldn't help the way it responded to my dedication to the gym. I told you I decided not to go through with it and you said, "Yeah, you don't need those, babe. You're perfect the way you are." Said the person who told me to get them in the first place! It was a classic play for a skilled manipulator - make me distrust myself to trust solely in you.

I was starting to lose it. I didn't know what was real. Who was I? I didn't even know the answer to that question anymore. I liked to do what you liked to do. I liked the music you liked. I felt how you felt. I gradually lost every sense of my identity in you. I walked in your shadow. I couldn't hear my own thoughts through the sound of your voice. I gave you the power to control me for so long, I felt like a brainless slave indebted to its "Massa." I lost my voice and my sense of humor, along with what was left of my mind. Even my naked body was draped in resentment.

It was easier for me to say nothing at all. I kept my thoughts and ideas to myself, in fear of you shooting them down as stupid like you routinely did. I hated you. I hated how you made me feel. I hated how you could do no wrong. I hated how the world revolved around you. I hated your sarcasm. I hated how loud your voice got when someone disagreed with you. I hated your judgmental views. I hated how entitled you felt. I hated your cheap cologne. I hated you with all my might. You beat me so low to the ground that I had no desire to stand again. I let you destroy my spirit.

Do you remember the first time you put your hands on me? Do

you remember how you pushed me out of the bed? Do you remember when you bruised my arms? I didn't forget; things like that never leave you. Disagreements turned into screaming matches, and screaming matches turned to irreversible setbacks. You told me I wasn't pretty without fake hair and eyelashes. It was such a specific insult that even in the heat of the moment, I knew you genuinely meant that. Your words pierced my heart, the same heart that was so desperately clinging onto you for dear life. Your words did more damage than your hands could have ever done. I wasn't even crying because you physically hurt me; I was crying because the life I dreamt of was crumbling before my very eyes. I crawled back into bed, silencing my cries and wiping the tears of the harsh reality of my sadness. I knew this was the beginning of the end, with this beginning being far from the end. You betrayed me, you betrayed my trust, and you betrayed our relationship. I always told myself if a man were to ever put his hands on me, I would walk away. But walk away and go where?

The next day when we got home, I removed my hoodie and saw the marks you left. My arms were sore but they didn't hurt as much as seeing that you didn't really love me. You saw what you had done and kissed my bruises, promising me that you were sorry. Didn't all relationships have ups and downs? I mean, they were fairly small bruises; it's not like you gave me a black eye. Maybe I was overthinking everything like I always did. Maybe I was going crazy. Maybe I wasn't as smart as I thought I was. Maybe I was the only problem here and you did everything right. If I only had the courage, maybe I would've left you right then...

We went up to Chicago one weekend for some much-needed fun. Sometimes you try to escape the problem, but until you fix it, the problem will always rear its ugly head back in your life. We got into an argument in the hotel room, this time in front of your friend Ryan. I was sick and tired of you yelling at me; I had enough of you disrespecting me. I reached my arm back and slapped you as hard as I could. I think both of us were pretty shocked. The shock quickly turned into retaliation. You grabbed me and shoved me to the floor. This time, I wasn't done with you - I was mad as hell. I picked up shoes from the ground and threw them at you, almost breaking the lamp in the hotel. Whenever you got angry, you would use those opportune moments to say how you truly felt about me. A lot of your comments would refer to my past; this time you called me a misguided whore that had racked up so many bodies at a young age. You said you should've never taken me seriously. Luckily, your friend was there to intervene. Otherwise, who knows how far it would've gone.

I had never in my life despised anyone like I did you. We would argue and make up. You'd storm out or I'd storm out. It became a routine for us. One particular argument when we made up shortly after stood out to me. You wanted to take a nap and asked me to come to lay down. I did, for the sake of not starting another argument, but the shit you kept putting me through was turning my heart to stone. It was the "same shit, different day" with us, and there was no sign of letting up. You fell asleep fairly quickly while I hadn't even so much as blinked. The whole time, I was watching you sleep. You were so peaceful when your mouth was shut. Who would've thought the seemingly perfect stranger who was now my boyfriend could be so terribly wrong for me? A resting monster in our bed, so vulnerable and unsuspecting.

The thought of killing you crossed my mind, but how would I do it? I didn't have enough strength to suffocate you with a pillow or choke you 'til the life escaped your eyes. What about a knife, I thought. I could slit your throat from ear to ear, leaving a bloody mess for your parents to discover. Perhaps stab you like I was trying to win a Wack-A-Mole contest? I wanted to make you hurt the way you made me hurt. I would've missed you too much to end it all. I loved you, but you weren't worth losing my freedom or sanity. I knew at that very moment if I didn't get out, I was going to kill you or you were going to kill me. Maybe you never felt that way, but I did. I didn't know what I was capable of but I knew if I was capable of thinking it, I was capable of anything.

There was a time when you made me the happiest girl in the world. It felt brief amongst what we had become. Remember when we slow-danced to Aerosmith's "Don't Want to Miss a Thing" in your brother's kitchen? When we went to Paris? When we rapped Eminem in the car? The money we made from the workout plans? Or when I bought you a car in my name that ultimately would fuck up my credit because you didn't want to make the payments? I did everything to prove my devotion to you while you barely did enough to try to keep me. I was the breadwinner who paid for everything. Remember when you told me I should treat myself for once, so we went Michael Kors and I spent $600? You told me "I deserved it," even though I had to ask for your blessings to spend the money in my account. What karmic debt was I paying for to deserve the likes of you?

Growing up, I never fantasized about the white picket fence, seeing how I never had a semblance of that. When I played with my Barbie doll, she never had a boyfriend but she did have a big Dreamhouse and drove a pink drop-top Mustang. I dreamt of being able to do everything on my own - my Aunt Cindy played a huge role in that. I wanted the same independence she had. She had her shit together without needing a man, and I always admired that.

Seeing the way men treated my mom was enough for me to never want to be dependent on a man. She gave them her power. Her interests varied, depending on the type of guy she was dealing with at the time. She would bend over backward for them, time after time again - like a slinky going down the stairs. I never understood why she didn't feel good enough the way she was for them. I hated every guy she chose. I knew they were going to use her up, throw her in the dumpster, only to never be heard from again. I didn't like the idea of getting attached to someone who wasn't going to be around for very long. I didn't want to turn out like my mom, but there I was, dependent on a man.

I saw a future with you, despite all the hate that rumbled in my encaged heart. We talked about having a big family together because that's what you wanted. As much as I thought I was in love with you, I couldn't envision ever having your kids. You were the closest person to me in my life, yet I felt like I was laying my head on the chest of a complete stranger every night.

Did you get tired of me? Did my consistency bore you? Did you not respect me because I did whatever it took to make you happy? Were my efforts amusing? Whenever you were ready to fuck, was my pussy not always dripping for you? Every part of my existence craved you. I craved you the most when you acted like you didn't really want me. I never grew out of the side-chick mentality, even when I no longer stood on the sideline. I was always fighting for your time, attention and care, only to be acknowledged when you felt like doing so. I was praying for the day you saw my heart for what it truly was and saw me the way I saw you. I was replaceable to you and I could see it all over your face. You always glorified women who had features I didn't. They couldn't love you like I did, so why wasn't I enough for you?

Throughout the course of our relationship, I was never very close to your mom, but when you went overseas, I made many attempts to build that relationship. One afternoon, I suggested that she and I grab dinner at a new spot not far from where we lived. We had a very honest discussion about my relationship with you and her marriage with your dad. There were eerie similarities that confirmed everything I already knew about you. You both talked down to us and belittled us, were controlling, arrogant and selfish. As much as your mom loved you, she gave me a fair warning not be fooled and end up like her, unhappily married. I was taken aback by her bold vulnerability. She said if she could do it all over again differently, she would. She explained how so many years invested with children made for a messy divorce that she didn't want to endure. She didn't want to give up her lifestyle; she wanted to retire without financial stress. That conversation changed everything for me.

All of the fighting and fussing we did both publicly and behind closed doors began to outweigh the good times. Everything got old, fast. I told you if we couldn't respect one another, we didn't need to be together. This was the final straw. We had a long talk about what we could do better, and I really thought you meant the things you said. We made positive changes that lasted for about two weeks before you reverted back to the person you had always been.

Despite the distance I created with my family and friends, I called my aunt one summer afternoon for advice. My aunt and I weren't as close then as we are now, but I knew she was the ear I needed. Outside on the deck of your brother's house, I cried to her, telling her that I knew deep down I had to break up with you. I didn't know how I was to plan my grand escape, but I knew I needed out. We switched the title of my car over to your name since you paid the remaining balance I owed on it, so I had no transportation. There were no shackles on my ankles, but I was enslaved mentally. I couldn't stand the thought of another second with you, but I knew I had to be strategic. Your family outnumbered me, I had no reinforcements, and I knew it wasn't going to be a simple goodbye. I wanted to give our love one last shot before taking action, so I did. I suited up and prepared for battle.

As my number of followers increased on social media, so did my opportunities. I was offered to do a cover shoot for a magazine based in LA, all expenses paid. I originally didn't want to go because you weren't here to travel with me, but you convinced me this was something I couldn't turn down. Traveling alone as a woman never seems wise, considering how we share this grand universe with an abundance of barbaric pigs who can't control themselves, but against my initial concerns, I didn't have anything to lose if it meant gaining freedom. Instead of a booking a hotel, the owner of the magazine came back suggesting I stay at his studio where another Instagram girl named Marie was living at the time. I was familiar with her prior, so after expressing my skepticism, she made me feel confident enough to decline the hotel. She was alive with all her limbs and I didn't want to be difficult. I was happy to just be in the mix.

I was running late for my flight that day because I wanted to be dolled up for when I landed in LAX. I wore my pink-striped sundress with my golden highlighted hair flowing down my back. I was California-ready. On my way to the security gate, I forgot about my taser located in the side pouch of my Michael Kors purse. Always trying to do right by the law, I notified TSA that I had no intention of carrying it through, but I didn't know the proper way to dispose of it. I should've just thrown it away. Two police officers, one a young female and the other an older male, confronted me. I was completely oblivious to the fact that tasers were illegal in this state. I explained that I solely had it for my protection, being a woman and frequently going places alone. My eyes started to fill with tears as I was explaining, knowing I was soon to miss my flight. I knew I would never forgive myself if I missed an opportunity of this magnitude.

The male officer lacked any ounce of empathy while the lady

cop watched in cold silence. I broke the law and I should've been punished, but the City of Angels had different plans for me. When the male officer walked away, I started hyperventilating, not knowing what was next to come. Being a privileged white man, he would never understand the struggle of being a woman. I knew he certainly wasn't going to help my case. The female officer asked about the nature of my trip to LA, and I managed to reply through my crocodile tears that I did fitness and was traveling to my first cover shoot. The male cop was on the phone in a separate area overlooking while trying to figure out what to do with me. The female officer looked me in my eyes and said, "If I let you go, you have to promise me you'll kill it. Now go and don't look back. RUN!" I thanked her and bolted off as quickly as my sandals permitted me to my gate with tears streaming down my cheeks. I made it just three minutes before they closed the gate door.

The female officer was also white. It just went to show that there are kind and unkind people of every shade out there. When you think you can generalize people, you will be proven wrong about them. Men will never understand how scary it is to be a woman, regardless if they have daughters or not. God works through people, and that day, he rolled up his sleeves for me. I had no idea this would be the most important flight I'd ever catch in my entire life.

It was a two-day shoot and on one of my first nights there, Marie asked if I wanted to go to a rapper's house party in the hills with a few other girls. I was trying to make friends and not be the odd girl out, so I accepted the invitation. Being in a relationship for so long, I never got out much or socialized with other people. I had a whole boyfriend; what business did it serve trying to be seen in a tight outfit to be lusted after by other men?

The whole night leading up to the party, you completely refuted the idea, but the reality was that you didn't want me to go without you. You didn't trust me because you didn't trust yourself. You insisted I do Worldstar Hip Hop, you pre-approved the majority of all the photos I uploaded, you used my picture to solicit threesomes - *what more did you want?* You contributed to all the attention I garnered, and you wanted to bitch about me going to a party? I didn't even know the rapper personally - they did. You asked for permission to fuck a bitch when you went to Florida, and I let you! Who was really the insecure one?

As we were pulling up to the house party, I lost service in the middle of our heated conversation. There was no reception in the hills, but as a first-timer in LA, I had no idea and it couldn't have been at a shittier time. I felt nauseous from my anxiety because I didn't know if I was still going to have a boyfriend once the night was over. If I knew you like I knew I knew you, I knew you were livid and shaking from anger. I knew what it was going to look like regardless, so I decided to make the most of it by having fun for once. It wasn't like I wanted to be with anyone else - I never did. I justified that this made up for all the events I missed in college. I deserved to enjoy myself too! When you're young and unwed, what else are you supposed to do?

I wasn't allowed to do anything without you, and that was the bottom line. You could do whatever the fuck you pleased while I had a strict set of rules I was to religiously follow like the Bible. I always stayed at home, yet I never dared to utter a word of disapproval in the things you wished to do. Who knows how many broads you fucked behind my back when you had bitches texting you at all hours of the night on the phone I paid for each month! Your social media accounts were poppin' because I was with you. These girls didn't like you for you, dummy; they wanted the life I had down to the dick I laid up with every night. All of those college years, it was all about you - the star player that everyone in town wished they knew. Teachers giving you higher grades for autographs, free meals wherever we went - the rules didn't apply to you. My identity was always limited to being in the shadow as your girlfriend. Let me tell you something about those tables: Once they turn, they motherfuckin' TURN. The internet saved my life. Ain't that some shit...

Our arguments were like rollover minutes; whatever topic we last ended on carried on to the next conversation. It was like the heartfelt discussion we had about respecting one another and making the necessary changes to make the relationship work never happened. That quickly, we were back to square one. In between looks for my photo shoot, I was checking my phone. The venom you so effortlessly spewed brought tears to my eyes. I could feel the water touch the band of my lash strip. I knew this wasn't the time to cry, but I did. You always knew which buttons to push; you knew just what to say to hurt my feelings. I gave you the key to unlock my heart just for you to learn my triggers and shoot me down. I trusted you with my life and you took advantage of the knowledge you had to shrink me to nothing.

The owner offered me a place in the studio to live alongside

Marie until I found my own. If he had never given me the option to stay, I would've returned to my life in Indiana, entangled in our web of chaos. As much as I loved you, Seth, I felt in my heart that if I stayed, it wouldn't end well for me. I feared for my life and my sanity with you. I was ready to stand up to you once and for all to claim my life back. I had never broken up with someone before, but I had no problem with typing the official break-up text. Shit comes easier when you've had enough. I finally had the brains to see, heart to believe, and the courage to make that leap.

Immediately, you rang my phone, suggesting that we should just take a break and let it breathe. You said you loved me and were willing to treat me like the princess I truly was. As much as I wanted to believe you, I knew that I never was a princess to you. I was your doormat, a cum rag, a humble servant of your selfish needs. I never was one for "breaks"; it was either all or nothing. I chose nothing. There are no "breaks" in true love. You don't get to decide when you feel like doing right by someone. You don't get to completely ignore them until you miss them. This is love - not a fucking video game console you can turn on and off as you please.

Over the next couple days, you sent me "good morning" texts I hadn't received in years, pictures of what you were doing throughout the day, and action shots from your game. It's incredible how the fear of knowing you're moments away from losing someone can impact your amount of effort. I found it rather pathetic, but almost comical in a deranged way. You can always expect miraculous things when a person senses you're over their shit. To see that you were capable of this effort the entire time, but chose to be a dickhead, just turned me off even more.

I didn't even bother replying to most of your texts. It was fun having the ball in my court and watching you squirm, trying to crack the code. You pleaded for me to answer at least one FaceTime call, so out of my good nature, I decided to grant you at least that. After I let it ring a few times, I finally accepted it to see the face of the person I thought was the love of my life fill the screen.

I didn't have anything to say, so I held my phone and stared back into your watering eyes. You broke down, promising that things were going to be different. I had to refrain from throwing up and wanting to hang up, so I let the diarrhea flow through the gaps of your teeth. It was great to see you feel something after all these years I spent with you, doing for you, as I survived on your courtesy crumbs. You starved me of your love, and I learned to be thankful for those crumbs. At least they were something, and something is better than nothing, right? Wrong.

I hadn't said a word. My gaze was cold to match my heart you turned to an icebox. I gave you everything I had and you took it all without blinking. I never wanted it to come to this, but the beautiful stranger I spotted in the gym years ago was only a hideous monster wrapped in pretty paper. I'm sure you thought your little performance would move me, but it didn't, not even in the slightest. For a person who once boasted about never having had his heart broken, I was thrilled to be the bitch to teach you a lesson you'd never forget.

You said I had a few days to make a decision. The irony about your delivery was that I had no desire to reconcile with a man who never respected me to begin with. Once you realized we really weren't getting back together, it's like a switch flipped in you. I had only packed clothing for the couple days I originally planned to be away, while my entire life and sentimental belongings were in the basement of your parents' house. I wish I would have gone back to get my stuff, but our split was too messy to risk catching a case from beating your mom's ass. Going out with a bang would've made for quite the ending, but I never went back. Instead of spending money on a ticket back to Indiana, I used that money towards the start of my new wardrobe. Your mom threw out the majority of my shit because she's always been a miserable cunt, but she did not discard my laptop and birth certificate per my threat to get the police involved. Thankfully, I managed to somehow make one friend who was willing to go pick up my things, seeing how your family thought they had the right to withhold my items since I was "evicted." My friend picked up the box your mom left on the doorstep a few weeks later, and once that happened, you texted me. You informed me that I was dead to your family. You told me I was never to speak to them again. That was actually one of the only things that made me cry, knowing I was losing a family I spent years with too.

Despite our challenges, I really grew to love them. Maybe not love, but I was able to maneuver around better within the household, which made my experience there more tolerable.

It was all for the best, considering there were other red flags that I could foresee as future problems. There was the time I heard

65

your dad describe your brother's girlfriend, who was black, as having "ape-like" features. Or maybe when you guys would quote "Django" and felt it was appropriate to include the n-word when re-enacting the scenes. What good is asking for the signs if you just ignore them? I was never really welcome. It was never meant for you to be mine forever.

You always said I was too into the lights but the lights chose *me*. Even when I was taking pictures in the basement, not knowing where it'd get me, I never lost hope. I saw more for myself even when I had nothing. I don't regret you, Seth; I loved you more than you'll ever know. I didn't make it down the aisle with you, but you were a stepping-stone to the path I was always destined to walk. The woman I dreamed of being is the woman I became. If I ever go looking for my heart's desire again, I won't look any further than my own backyard, because if it isn't there, I never really lost it in the first place.

EVAN
Flag On The Play

After Seth, I felt like I was drunk, falling out of love trying to find my Uber. I was numb, from my heart to my feet. I knew when the sun peeked its head from behind the horizon because that's when I would again feel the pain I was trying to escape. I suffered night terrors for months. I would wake up out of my sleep sweating, crying, enraged - or all three if I was lucky. I had been so accustomed to being cuddled every night that I couldn't fall asleep without the presence of a pillow close to me like a warm body. I was withdrawing from love with no medical assistance. I was on my own to get through this, and Dr. Renner had her work cut out for her.

All of the time I spent in the gym and perfecting my regimented diet went out the window once I became newly single. In my relationship with Seth, I felt so pressured to be perfect that I was repulsed by the thought of continuing what he instilled in me. It just reminded me of how he controlled me, from bitching about me eating Oreos, to not getting low enough in my squat. I dismissed any memory pertaining to my old life and I decided I wanted to do things my way for a change.

When I finally found the strength to make it to the gym, I had lost most of my abs, my butt had shrunk, and I couldn't keep any weight on because I had no appetite. I broke down on my second set and started crying mid-Bulgarian split squat while listening to Eminem's "25 to Life." My entire existence was so heavily influenced by him that I felt clueless trying to function alone in society. I didn't know who I was, what I liked, or what the hell I even planned to do with my life.

I couldn't stomach the thought of his absence, let alone comprehend what I was feeling. I just wanted the pain to go away. Instead of identifying the symptoms and finding a remedy, I hopped to the next dick without hesitation. I started to see how Jean must've felt. Be careful for what you wish for, right? With my rising appeal on social media, the possibilities were endless. The people who I couldn't entertain while I was in a committed relationship were now free-game. I had no business dating anyone at that time, but I was sick with spite. The turnaround time for how quickly I moved on would've been upsetting for any ex, but that was the point. I wanted Seth to hurt, which brings me to you, Evan.

We were ironically in the same area the first time we met. You were staying in Thousand Oaks while I was in the heart of downtown LA. The Uber ride to your address was expensive but worth it to meet you. Physically, you were every shallow trait I ever desired in a man. I should've known after you said you had only slept with 25 girls in your lifetime – which was clearly a lie - that I was wasting my time from the jump. Why go out of your way to be untruthful, adding insignificant details when you could've refused to answer the question or just told the truth. I guess that's what dating consists of for anyone, lies in the beginning until you get them where you want them. I was young-minded and fresh out of a situation where "body count" mattered, which is why I asked. In truth, it shouldn't matter at all. Due to my lack of any potential prospects lined up and having nothing better to do with my time, getting out there again felt better than confronting the pain of the past.

When discussing future travel plans, you informed me if I wanted to see you that I had to buy my own ticket. You convinced me that this was a test to gauge my true intentions and interest. You had just signed a monstrous deal and knew you were on the radar for women looking to hit big. You said that if I was in it for the right reasons, I would put the money up, so I did. I had my own, and I knew my heart; I didn't see the issue with proving my loyalty. I was already in over my head. I used my own hard-earned money, a financial cushion I had no business shelling out to make this relationship work.

I was a naive girl with a very old-fashioned perspective on dating that didn't apply to what I had signed up for. I walked into a slaughterhouse with the hopes of a fairytale ending. From Day 1 of your dry texting to our spontaneous monthly encounters, you were always very robotic. I thought you were either an asshole or extremely guarded, but it was just your stale personality. When we spent time together, looking at you felt like looking in the mirror. I don't think either of us really understood how much we had in common.

I was your best-kept secret. You hid me away like a

community whore, all while I would stay with you for days at a time, making your bed each morning. Your forehead kisses always woke me up before you went off to practice. I even helped you unpack your kitchen when you moved into your new house overlooking the peaceful city. Why were you ashamed of me?

I remember you asked me one evening, "What's your pinnacle?" And I didn't know what the fuck "pinnacle" even meant. I hadn't even bought my ticket back home yet, but you expected me to know what I wanted to accomplish the most in life? I knew in your own way, you were searching for answers because you cared about me. You wanted me to be so much further along than I was, and there was nothing I could do about it. Truth is, I had much to resolve that I didn't attempt to tend to; I was content with the money I was making from Instagram and the freedom of being able to jump on a late flight to see you.

Sex with you was new and fun, but once the newness wore off, it quickly grew redundant. You always ended with doggy style for the finisher. You didn't challenge me sexually, but your body was a work of art I enjoyed penetrating me. Our bond blossomed slowly, but the slow progress was still progress in my mind. I traveled to a couple of your away games before you eventually decided to invite me to my first home game. It's hard keeping a low profile when you have thousands of followers checking for your profile. A few people recognized me at the game in the family/girlfriend section and asked for some selfies. I was new to this and oblivious to the trail I was leaving for wandering eyes to find. You guys won your game and wanted an intimate celebration, so we all met up at your friend's apartment afterward. I was excited to finally be included after months of sneaking around. I knew this was your way going out on a limb to show me that you were trying to give me a chance.

The feelings I still harbored for Seth, I projected onto you. Not projection in the sense of being accusatory or jaded, but I projected all the love I had stored for him onto you. I had been drinking heavily since he and I parted ways. I thought I was invincible, even though addiction runs in my family. I wanted to erase what my heart wouldn't allow me to forget. That night, I took six shots of Patron and smoked until feeling nothing throughout my body.

That night, I showed my ass, perhaps literally and figuratively. It was all a blur, but I remembered twerking in front of your friends, even though I said I don't dance. Shortly after, I ran into the screen door I could've sworn looked open. I didn't cross my mind how wild I looked because I was too fucked up to care. As if I didn't embarrass myself enough, the car ride home was the icing on the cake. I told you that I didn't want people to know about our us either because if they knew, it would lower my stock. You took your eyes completely off the road and glared over at me in utter disbelief. There was nothing but crickets the whole way back after that. I shocked myself by my statement, considering you had millions of dollars and power on a level I wasn't anywhere near matching.

When we pulled up to the house, I began to realize the extent of the damage I had done, so I was determined to make it all better by having sex. You might've been mad, but what guy wouldn't still want to get his rocks off? Your ego fucked me rough that night. It wasn't the most ideal circumstances, but your aggressive energy was a nice change of pace from the usual. Before I got out of the car to catch my flight, I asked when I was going to see you again. You replied, "What I want to do and what I'm going to do are two different things. That's all I'm going to say." For someone who acted so shaken up, you still chose to have sex with me, so I brushed off the petty riddle. I didn't hear back from you for weeks, and it all pretty much went downhill from there.

During our time apart, you got caught up on multiple occasions with other women in the blogs. Whenever I asked you about it, you'd mockingly deny it, even though anyone with eyes could see it was clearly you. When we'd argue, you just blamed me for the state of how things were. You tried to open up to me and look where it got you, you'd say. In all actuality, those inches we made were miles long in your eyes.

You were barely giving me anything to work with - text after text after text, just to get no response. A person can only do so much before you start looking like a fucking lunatic. My ego was large and in charge; it wouldn't let me see the error in my ways. If I couldn't get shit from you emotionally, I planned to find it elsewhere. It was getting too expensive to see you, and I was fed up with your unwillingness to budge. I didn't even have my own apartment yet; I was spending what could've been rent money to see you. It wasn't adding up, so we became divided. Everybody loses when games are played.

You served as the greatest rebound of all time. You were the prime example of how looks and money can't make up for a subpar personality and the inability to be close to people due to past traumas. Pot, meet kettle! I'm surprised we weren't more compatible. My parents didn't give a fuck about me either. It's a gut-wrenching feeling knowing the people who took part in creating you want nothing to do with you. I felt adopted too. I was in search of a love I never had, but I knew there were missing pieces to my puzzle. We can hate our parents, but we still carry on their shortcomings if we don't resolve our conflicts with them in ourselves. You left without a proper goodbye before I had the chance to say "thank you" for being the best-timed distraction. I never once thought about getting back with Seth because I had you. It wasn't long before I dashed off into the arms of someone else in the same fashion I did with you. I tried to self-medicate without knowing the proper diagnosis. I didn't have any problems and that became the problem.

LEON
Soul Tie With A Songbird

When you first tried reaching out to me, I blew you off. I knew you did that kind of thing often so I was unimpressed. After a little persistence on your end, we eventually exchanged numbers. I thought your random FaceTime calls were incredibly obnoxious but it didn't stop me from answering. I think my initial lack of interest aroused you. There's nothing more enticing than a "no" in your world full of people who typically say "yes." You were charming and even when I was a smartass, you'd respond with something clever to make me smile. I could see how the challenge ignited a flame in your eyes.

I didn't want to fall for someone like you, but the more I tried to fight it, the more interested I became. My curiosity and your way with words brought my guard down with ease. I was only seeing Evan at the time but you took me away from him. You were the emotional stimulation I was so desperately seeking. When things got rocky between he and I, there you stood, cape blowing in the wind to save the day. Options create choice; choice creates freedom. I knew I had you and naturally stopped caring about Evan at all. The random FaceTime calls turned to texts, texts turned to hours of phone calls, and phone calls turned to a real connection. Remember when we were on the phone until 7:00am? You shared a lot about yourself that morning, intimate details that you claimed to not typically share, but you trusted me.

One night, we were on FaceTime talking about the usual and you making me laugh at senseless things. Mid-conversation, you pulled out your dick and there was your penis plastered on the entire screen. I had been with a few guys but was still very much inexperienced. I was so caught off guard that I couldn't find enough words to formulate a complete sentence. You began stroking it with this hypnotic gaze in your eyes, the same look I often saw when your wheels were turning. I wasn't sure what to do. Was this the part when I started touching myself too? Do I just look and moan? We never spoke sexually; we hadn't even met in person yet. Although our attraction towards one another was evident, it just wasn't like that. After what felt like the longest minute, I suggested it was time to get off the phone. You had implanted this erasable, burning image in my virgin eyes. You did just enough to get my imagination going, and I think that was your main objective. You could tell I didn't want you to stop; I just didn't know how to say it. Mission accomplished.

Time only brought us closer. We shared a lot about ourselves. I cried to you about Seth and you listened. You always had a way of comforting me; you became my confidant. I felt like we just clicked, maybe because we were soulmates in a past life - if you believe in that sort of thing. You were adamant about meeting face-to-face at whatever cost. I, on the other hand, was hesitant because our chemistry over the phone was so undeniably strong that I knew it would only lead to one thing in person. You made me feel like goo, giggling like a little school girl on the phone. I didn't want to just be another girl in your bed; I wanted to mean something to you. I didn't know how I planned to differentiate myself from the rest, but I was confident in my heart. I knew when it came to sex, I was lightyears behind in comparison, but if one person was going to bring me up to speed, it would be you.

I loved the role you played in my life too much to rush anything and jeopardize losing you. I avoided seeing you like the plague at first until I couldn't handle being apart for another second. I had an event in Texas the following weekend. You said whether I liked it or not, you were coming and I could stop by the hotel if I changed my mind about seeing you. I didn't think you were crazy enough to go through with it, but you did. That evening before I was scheduled to be at the venue, I met you and brought a friend so I wasn't alone. You always gave the best hugs. They were warm and intoxicating.

You ended up accompanying me at my hosting that night, along with your security to ensure a smooth operation. Get the money, get in, and get out. I felt safe with you. You were extremely protective of me and I loved that about you. Nobody ever gave me that feeling before. After the event, we went back to your room where we even took a couple selfies to send my mom. She knew how much I gushed about you even when I wasn't able to admit to you or myself how highly I thought of you. We hopped in the bed and went right to sleep.

I was shocked. Were you actually in this for me? Instead of catching my flight home, you suggested I fly back with you to spend more time together. I didn't want to because I so badly wanted to believe I was in control. Everything felt right, almost making it impossible to say no. We were shoulder to shoulder on the flight, joking about the GoGo WiFi. The few days we shared consisted of charity work, laughs, and confirming what I had such difficulty professing. I couldn't get enough of you.

Your love was one of the most potent drugs with which I had ever experimented. I would soak in each letter from every word, wide-eyed, taking in their detail like I was on an everlasting Adderall pill. You were my best friend. When I'd travel alone to my different hostings, you'd have your friends in that city act as my security. You were the first guy to ever send me flowers, three dozen beautiful red roses. You made me feel special in more ways than one in such a short amount of time. I learned that the length of a relationship doesn't equate to closeness; the depth of it determines that. I felt more attached to you than I did in all the years I spent with Seth. Seth didn't know my ins and outs. He didn't ask me questions. He stopped wanting to learn about me after he got me. It was the little things with you that went a long way. "You see a side of me not many get to see," you said. Despite your history and playboy bravado, I always saw your heart of gold shining through any uncertainty. You just needed someone to value it more than they did the bullshit that followed you. The rumors regarding your sexuality never bothered me. True or not, it didn't make me love you any less.

Before we were ever intimate, I had hope for what was to come of our relationship. I thought I could spend my life with you, well, that's how you made me feel at least. I could've thrown in the towel and never looked back for you. You were everything and more I wanted packaged into one mesmerizing human. There was nobody else but you. I felt like the luckiest girl in the world. You made me feel like my life and presence in your life mattered. I was convinced that sharing all the painful things I had been through, you would never let me down the way everyone else did.

You had my mind tightly wrapped up like a cocoon. It was months before we had sex for the first time, but it was well worth the wait. You don't have the slightest clue what you're missing until you get it, and once you get it, you can't live without it. Each touch, each moan, each position - it's like you mastered sex. As if we weren't obsessed with each other enough, sex sealed the deal. I blame you for the start of what would soon become my sexual deviance. You navigated my body effortlessly. You did things to me I didn't even know I would like.

The second time was the most memorable for me. My pussy was throbbing at the thought of you being inside me again when you were just lying next to me. Any innocence I had remaining, you robbed from me. I never thought I'd be the type to find pleasure in being choked and slapped, but because it was you, I was with it. You liked seeing how far I would let you take it. I didn't expect to be so turned on by you grabbing my face and spitting in my mouth just to suck it all back up and finish with a long sloppy kiss. I'm pretty sure when your mouth engulfed mine you took a part of my soul with you.

Even though we only had sex twice, it was so easy to cum simply by reminiscing about it. I loved how nasty you'd get and vocal you were about what felt good. Your tone of voice would shift when you were getting in gear to have sex. I loved your voice, my little songbird. I'm pretty sure I just loved everything about you at one point. I gave you a hard time because you could do no wrong in my eyes, and that was frightening.

As much as I would've liked to put my full trust in you, you wanted me to accept the fact that you were fucking other women. On one occasion, you thought you were doing me a favor by forewarning me that you had six bitches coming back to the room for group play. Your reasoning for being so open was because you wanted to be honest with me. Honesty is great but it isn't magic. How did you expect a truth like that to be overlooked when I had these deep feelings for you? Why would I ever condone you having meaningless sex with girls that you didn't really care about? If you had me, why did you need them?

Evidently, I didn't impact your life as much as you claimed I did, seeing how you resorted back to your same shit. The walls I let down for you started making their way back up, and you noticed the change. You always got angry when you knew I was upset. The connection we worked diligently to establish began to deteriorate with each argument. For every snide remark and unfair accusation, I had the perfect reply. At one point, you sent me fifteen text messages in a row, and I would always turn right back around to match it. I hated it just as much as you did, but you never wanted to hear my point of view. I loved you like I knew you wanted to love me.

Mountain highs and valley lows became our consistently inconsistent cycle. You let us go months without speaking and then you'd pop back in like you didn't just disappear on me without a trace. You blamed me for your distance; you blamed me for the demise of us. You wanted me to love you while you made every decision parallel to breaking my heart. I hated how fond I grew of you. You always claimed that I wanted you to be this perfect man, but that was never the case. I thought you were perfect the way you were; I just wanted you to treat me better. I knew better. Anyone in search of perfection will spend forever and a day trying to find it. The only thing I ever believed to be perfect was the idea of you and me together.

You began to mentally and emotionally drain me. You never followed through with the things you said you'd do, and if we got too close, you would run away. You were the one who told me the only thing constant in life is change, yet nothing about you was willing to change. Why were you so unwilling to hold yourself accountable? I was "the angel on your shoulder" yet you often flicked me off of it. You never took my feelings into consideration when you didn't agree with them. We never got back on track; you were scared and so was I. I felt like I was chasing a mirage, hoping for the day you could be honest with yourself and your feelings about me. You can never expect someone to keep it real with you when they don't keep it real with themselves. Broken promises lead to irreparable damage.

We tried time after time again to be casual, but it was never casual with you. You couldn't stand the thought of seeing me with someone, so you kept your distance without letting me get too far. You let a person you know gave a fuck walk away, but you couldn't let go of empty sex with empty people. Maybe I should've trusted my intuition or my aunt when she said you were another player dealing another game of manipulation. Where there's smoke, there's fire, and only you can prevent forest fires. My guard wasn't up for no reason. If you didn't fit the description outsiders tried to paint onto you, who were you? Maybe I was foolish for believing in the person I saw looking back at me. Was anything real? Did you mean any of the shit you said or were those just classic ploys you used on everybody? You cared so much about me but never enough.

Maybe I could have been more open. Maybe I was *too* open. Maybe I should've told you how much you meant to me when I was being dismissive. Maybe it was a good thing I didn't let you know everything you made me feel. Maybe I was too harsh. Maybe you weren't willing to see where you were at fault. Maybe it was my entire fault. What if you were wrong? Can you live with knowing we might never know "what if?"

To this day, you say you were all about me when it wasn't all about me. It was all about you, and you wanted me to be okay with putting my feelings second to yours. That's not love - that's selfishness. All the years I spent with Seth, and he couldn't compare to you. As much as I wanted it to work with Evan, he wasn't you. There was nobody like you, and in the same breath, nobody has ever disappointed me as much as you did.

If someone is a good person sometimes but a bad person most of the time, what does that make them? Human? Or scum? Everyone has the ability to be a good person all the time, but do we excuse their behavior when they frequently choose not to be? Any person who has ever had quality would never value quantity. Any person who says one thing but does another is full of shit. Love doesn't hurt - it heals. Self-love cannot be optional because it is imperative for survival.

I'm sure you made a lot of girls feel the way I did. The thing with guys like you is they never have any intention of changing, just finding new victims. Once the puppy becomes an adult and is able to see the truth for what it is, you abandon them. The ride never ends with you until the other person decides to get off. You are the type of person who will always be around if permitted, never any different but expecting different treatment. No woman alive can change a man, no matter how beautiful, rich, intelligent or tolerant she may be. A man who sees no fault in his way of living doesn't see beyond the horizon. It's not personal.

I never stopped loving you; I just loved me more than the idea of you.

සා ✿ ශ්‍ර

FRANK
One And Done

I have always been friendly but I never had many friends. The same girl I mentioned in Seth's chapter, Marie, became one of my close friends. She would go out to enjoy the nightlife quite a bit, but my loner nature kept me inside unless I had a personal interest in going, which was a rarity. It was cool having someone to talk to about the struggles of dating and to accompany on runs to Starbucks. We didn't have much in common from an intellectual standpoint, but she was well-connected.

Marie was talking to a young guy fresh on the scene and spent most of her time with him. She said I should get out of the house for once and have fun. She was trying to hook me up with her guy's friend since they were signed under the same agency.

I took one glance at your Instagram account and you just looked like you ain't shit. You seemed way too into yourself and entirely too young at that. What in the entire fuck could a young idiot with money do with a complex woman like me? I objected to the idea as absurd.

G'day Frank! Fancy seeing you in here mate! It all started with a Snapchat you sent me from an account belonging to a mutual friend. I finally got Marie off my back about you, but I guess she didn't have the heart to deliver the message. As sure as I felt about the unlikelihood of this potentially illogical union, there was something about our virtual exchange that intrigued me. Maybe it was your shameless attempt to contact me or the fact that you didn't give up easily. We exchanged numbers and the rest was history. For the first couple weeks, we were both glued to our phones overstimulated and hungry for more. Our conversation flowed with ease for such a gap in age. We were able to relate on more levels than I had originally expected. It's crazy how when you first get to know a person, they're a complete stranger that can suddenly mean everything to you. That's how it happened with you, Frank. I had gone out on several unsuccessful dates and short-lived situationships since Leon but hadn't come across anyone I really liked until I met you. God brought us together for a reason.

One week I'm in Mississippi visiting my friends, smiling from ear to ear while texting you, and the next week, I'm at home walking outside to the car you sent for me. You FaceTimed me to make sure I got in safely and even warned the driver to be careful with your "precious cargo." It was almost like a modern-day fairy tale of a prince fetching his princess. Except this princess didn't dance the night away and leave when the clock struck midnight; she stayed the night and was DTF because she was grown.

We became close fairly quickly. I wanted you to know everything about me so nobody would be able to tell you something you didn't already know. When we got on the subject of previous partners, I didn't shy away from the whole truth. I wasn't ashamed of the guys I had been with and had nothing to hide. On the other hand, it was never your fucking business to begin with, but I was comfortable with my truth. I pride myself on being an honest person in a day and age when that's considered a superpower.

At the time, you seemed accepting of the choices I made prior to you, but I couldn't have been more wrong. The male ego is fragile like the ball sack that hangs between their legs. There's more than one way to bring a man to his knees so you can get creative, which would be more effective to attack depending on the circumstances. I don't regret not lying to you; it just should've never mattered who I was with before you.

Our age wasn't the issue as much as our personality differences. I was surprised I made you laugh as much as I did. You were serious most of the time while I would purposely do sporadic things to see your reaction. I think you liked my eccentric personality in contrast to yours. I didn't understand your dry humor at first but you grew on me. Where you were my calm, I was your chaos.

The first time we had sex, I almost shed a tear of joy when I saw the size of your dick. The reveal, in general, is nerve-racking and the stakes are heightened when you already like the person and feel like the sex just has to check out. You didn't know what to do with that thing, but luckily, you were in good hands. I overlooked the little shit I noticed along the way because of our unquestionable chemistry. Blinded by love? Or blinded by the cock? Sex can be blinding and binding when you both actually like each other.

I was never a fan of giving head. It always felt degrading being down on the same knees I used to pray. It didn't help that my jaw would always get tired or try to lock up after two minutes. My aunt always joked about how men ranked good dick suckers higher than good women more times than none. Perhaps that was why I was still single. Who wants to commit to a girl who can't suck them dry of common sense? I took it upon myself to invest time learning how to suck it like a porn star - the only Trump I support, to be exact. Teanna Trump's relentless energy was second to none! I can't recall a moment that she ever looked like she would prefer air over taking her last breath to gag on the dick. I admired her passion and wanted to bring those same elements to my head game. I studied video after video and it was time to get some experience in the field. Before you knew it, you couldn't get enough of me. We were one another's kryptonite. It felt good indulging in all that bad with you. It was nothing for me to go above and beyond for you because you sold me the best dream, a dream you had no intention of bringing to fruition. But you made it sound good, so I bought it and got the second one free.

Your mask began to slip more and more frequently, exposing your true self. You were pretty demanding but since your voice wasn't loud, it never seemed like it. You'd make subtle remarks about my clothes and the amount of makeup I'd wear. You made passive aggressive comments whenever the subject of my social media arose. The longer I stayed around, the more condescending you became. You threw things I did in the past before you in my face like I wasn't the one who told you. Every guy was my "little boyfriend," followed by a cry of insecurity that got old fast.

They say do not trust all men, but trust men of worth; the former course is silly, the latter a mark of prudence. I trusted you, and just that quickly, you let me know I wasn't emotionally safe with you. Nothing brought about this change; it was just who you were. My heart = was too big to fit on a sleeve, so I sure knew how to entice energy vampires. You can't necessarily control what ends up on your doorstep because plenty of sociopaths want to use and abuse good people, but you can control what you let in.

Someone took footage of us at the mall and it hit the blogs the next day. To see my name attached to every word synonymous with "slut" hurt my feelings. It hurt me because it painted me as the villain. The name-calling was unnecessary but I learned a long time ago I was an easy target for the media. There are perks to being classified as a villain because the pressure isn't as high to be perfect. Villains are the ones who know the most and care the least - that's why they are feared. My fragile heart and genuine intentions didn't matter because those labels told the world all they needed to know about me. I was villain-tagged; there was never going to *not* be a negative perception painted about me. I knew you weren't ready for the scrutiny that this new territory required. I knew it wasn't going to be long before I lost you.

I saw you fighting to separate, knowing I was a good person, and yet, hearing what people were saying. I thought you saw me for who I was, but the things everyone told you must not have been too far off from what you already thought about me. We got along when you weren't being an insecure prick. Neither one of us could deny the feelings we had. I pity the fool who sees perception as reality; you miss a lot of depth that way. Your team ordered you to "burn the witch" and sunset was upon us. How was I the witch when I only had eyes for you? I never wanted or needed shit from you. I trusted you with my heart to only have you drop it on the carpet and hand it back covered in dirt and hair. You were the fool and that made me just as much of a fool as you.

I'm not embarrassed to say you crushed my heart in the hotel room the day you officially broke things off. I cried and you hugged me to console me. Your embrace didn't make me feel any better because I knew it was only temporary. After you let go, you told me that it wasn't possible to have everything I wanted due to the life I chose and everything that came with it. I looked at you in horror, mortified that you actually believed that nonsense. Why do I have to settle when I can have it all? I refused to accept that love couldn't be in my cards simply because a few people knew my name. What's meant for you will always be for you.

We still kept in contact for as long as I could handle it. I felt stupid yet again for thinking you'd be any different than the rest. I captioned every picture with a cryptic message to release the anger I had boiling inside me. Nobody was #TeamBrittany, and when you've never hurt anyone, it's a bitter horse pill to swallow. One of your siblings took to Twitter to call me "Bundle of Thottany," like I wasn't talking to her about ab exercises on FaceTime just months prior. I couldn't understand where this hatred was coming from because I didn't understand the magnitude of my power.

We had sex a couple more times, but the curtains closed for good when you told me one of your siblings tried to commit suicide in spite of us reuniting again. They saw our connection as a threat to their relationship with you. I didn't take you away from anything; you're the one who pulled me in but it still fell back on me. I learned from my first experience with Seth's ex Jean that this was bigger than trying to retaliate against Twitter fingers. I wouldn't be shocked if you even lied about that too, but I didn't want to be the reason someone took their own life. As much as it pained me to let you go, I cooperated.

I never defended myself because I didn't want you to have any additional drama that stemmed from me. I cared about you more than pleasing my ego. Our situation never sat right with me. From strangers to being inseparable, and back to like we were strangers all over again. Where are the feelings supposed to go when a relationship ends? Do they ever go away when it's real? When do feelings outweigh the opinions of others? I know you still think of me, I know you miss what we had.

You judged me even after I was vulnerable with you. And you didn't stop me from walking out of the room that day. How much did you like me if you wanted me to condense the very things that made me, me? Or change anything for that matter? There were plenty of signs but I thought if I modified parts of me, I had a better chance to be seen as girlfriend material.

If a person wants you to change for any purpose other than the betterment of yourself, you could never be the one for them. When you see a flower you marvel at it, water it, contribute to its growth where needed, but you never pluck it to possess it. There is no desire to change the size, shape, or color because it's beautiful just as you found it. Nobody gets to criticize a sunflower for not being a rose. If they want a rose, they need to go get a rose and leave the sunflower the fuck alone. Love uplifts - it doesn't pick apart. I never wanted to change you; I just wanted you to see the real beauty I housed internally. My heart was a greenhouse; you wouldn't know by the outside looking in what I had to offer unless you opened the door.

ജ ✿ ര

IVAN
Use Your Head

After all the apparent dickheads I was attracting, I figured I needed to formulate a new plan. Something had to give. I wanted to be able to confidently say all guys weren't bad, but the jury was still out on that one. Maybe I was missing out on all the nice guys because I liked the thrill of the chase, inconsistency and emotional abuse. Every single man I encountered had been so accustomed to women throwing themselves at them that unless they could spot the difference, they'd never know the difference. I didn't know if I needed to mentally prepare to fuck myself until the end of time, get out there again to date – a.k.a. getting humped and dumped some more - or accept that the concept of love was all a lie.

One day as I was casually scrolling through my DMs, one profile, in particular, caught my eye. After a further detailed investigation, I came to the conclusion that Momma liked what she saw. He was a lowkey athlete who was known, but nobody would recognize him outside of his game uniform. Hello again Ivan! You didn't have many posts and weren't following any of us IG girls, with the exception of me. We exchanged numbers because you were fine as hell and looked like everything I had been missing. We talked all throughout the day aside from when you had practice or treatment. You were sweet and consistent. We talked about dreams, conspiracy theories, why we thought we were single, and how we coped with the loss of a family member.

You were almost too laid-back, but with my being so high-strung, it balanced out. I never felt any real sparks between us, but you were more reliable than the men I dealt with before you. After a few weeks of constant communication, you came out and told me you had a daughter. It wasn't a deal breaker, but I questioned why you waited so long to tell me. You explained that you wanted to get a feel for me before opening up about it since that part of your life wasn't on public display. I felt like we reached some kind of milestone in our relationship where you wanted to see how long I was going to stick around.

You flew me to Boston shortly after that to watch you play. As my plane began to descend, the city looked like the inside of a snow globe. I'm not sure where your head was, but I wasn't taking a long flight just to fuck. I could've stayed in LA and made some phone calls for that. This was me accepting your invitation to see if you had anything to offer other than hard dick and bubble gum. The chemistry we had over the phone translated to the chemistry we had once we got in person. We sat and talked for hours. You were even more playful in person. I genuinely felt comfortable around you and I could tell you did too. We couldn't resist the magnetic pull that finally brought us close enough together to cuddle.

I've been with plenty of guys that only wanted sex. You don't have to be a mathematician to put two and two together. With the few exceptions, most guys weren't trying to discuss the moon and stars; they just got straight to it. I was completely thrown off when I heard you say you didn't want a serious relationship. You weren't looking for a girlfriend, but you pretty much had been treating me like that was my title all along. Whenever a man says he doesn't want a relationship, he just means he doesn't want a relationship with *you*. Believe him. If he was on the fence about it, why would he rule it out if those feelings were there?

I wanted to change up my typical procedure, so I went into the situation with no intention of having sex. My goal was to appear wholesome. I thought I could possibly change the outcome if I gave off a different perception. It was the last day of my cycle anyway and to save myself from any potential embarrassment, I stuck a plug up there to avoid any temptation. Nothing is sexy about a guy trying to stick his fingers in your pussy when you know your insides are bleeding out of your vagina.

We had a lot of organic sexual chemistry, and if I wasn't so fixated with my new approach, I probably would've let you beat. Of course me being me, I couldn't even fake having a lick of class without leaving you with something to remember. I didn't have to suck your dick, but I wanted to because once you get the hang of it, it becomes an art. I was glad I didn't waste a body when I saw what you were working with down there. My walls would've been furious, side-eyeing me with every stroke.

For all the men who have small penises, keep calm…we know it's out of your control. Just don't give a bigger ego than your dick. Now you know how we women feel about our body parts. No, size isn't everything, but it is to some. If you know the secrets to the woman's anatomy, you'll have any dime looking up at you while gagging on your 5-inch. I don't discriminate, but I can admit to having a weakness for a Lysol can. I would have a much shorter list if I had X-ray vision - let's just say that. I knew making you cum would be a walk in the park from the way your body surrendered. I don't know if all women feel like this, but I can sense intimidation like a great white shark sniffs out blood miles away. The plus about guys with shmeats is you can make them disappear with ease like Houdini with tits.

You came quickly, to no surprise; it's always a compliment when you can do your one job well. You see the fickle games my mind plays? One minute, I swear I'm holding out. The next, I'm on my knees showcasing the corruption behind my eyes.

You had to go back to your room for curfew so our time was cut short for the night. We texted back and forth but I didn't see you the rest of the time I was there. You didn't stop by after team breakfast or your meeting. You left your schedule in my room, so I knew exactly where you were and when you had free time. Being game day, I didn't think much of it. I was enjoying myself running up the room service tab and watching movies. You got me a great seat to the game, so there wasn't much else I could've wanted.

The game was intense and my seat was even closer than I anticipated. I had an amazing time but I was ready to go home. The whole situation was weird, seeing how you flew me out there to not even really see me or try to fuck me. It was your money, so I didn't dwell long on it.

I'd be lying if I said I was prepared for you to "ghost" on me once I made it back to LA. Your responses became more infrequent, shorter, and eventually stopped altogether. We didn't even have sex, so what was the issue? I was tired of letting these men off the hook so easily, so I confronted you over text about you switching up. I refused to let this awkwardness linger any longer.

Your first response was to try to avoid the question altogether by acting like you didn't know what I was talking about. Typical. Let's try this again. I was so direct in my response that I left no room for a riddle. On the second attempt, you gave me a real answer, the type of answer I was looking for the first time. You said that you weren't looking for a relationship and I was a relationship-type girl.

I didn't press you for a relationship or give you some ultimatum. I never talked about anything beyond what was going on that day with you; it was never a situation I pictured futuristically. I was simply getting to know you because that's what you do when you're single. I took a five-hour flight to not get fucked, give you head, for you to mentally check out before we were wheels down on the runway at LAX. It could've been worse. You could've wasted my time or left my text unanswered, but you answered honestly when you had no obligation to me. I will take a bitter truth over the sweetest lie any day of the week.

Getting your feelings hurt, even if it's by a guy you didn't really like can make anyone feel insecure. It's easy to feel undeserving, but you can't expect a hug from a pigeon. It's not that you aren't worthy of a hug, but the pigeon is simply incapable of giving you what you're asking for. Too many times, we allow a man's desire - or lack thereof - to define our value. Never confuse what you're offered with what you're worth. Nobody can take your worth away unless you put it in their hands yourself.

This experience assured me I was headed in the right direction for the type of guy I ultimately wanted. Nice guy or fuck boy, you cannot expect people to value the things they're unable to see. They can't appreciate what they can't differentiate.

SOLOMON
Malpractice

My plan needed a different direction. A smaller fish in the same pond wasn't enough; I needed to think beyond the confines of what I knew to explore the unknown. I had a rather peculiar DM that I originally ignored, make its way back around for a second shot. After all the failed situations, I found myself admiring the simplicity of your courage. I wanted so badly to give up on the idea of love ever finding me, but then there was you.

Salutations Solomon, I'm sure you are appalled that you made it in here, but that should serve as no surprise. You were charismatic at its finest, putting your fancy education to good use with your extensive vocabulary. I knew your game without ever picking up the sticks. If you ever intended on breaking into this castle, you were going to have to bring the militia. I would text you "good morning" just to leave your detailed response on "read" status. I was testing your temperament, the size of your ego, and the lengths you'd go to get to know me.

I would chuckle at your attempts but your double texts showed character. It takes a certain kind of person to continue being eager to try after being toyed with intentionally. Why was I giving you such a rough time? Outside of naturally having my guard up, in the back of my mind, I knew you had dated a former friend, Eliza. I originally met you through her at the Hollywood Hookah on one of the few occasions I went out. When she and I were cool, I honored our friendship; I didn't even see you in that light. I felt like my loyalty to her was one-sided, but I never confronted her about the shady things I noticed. None of my other friends liked her, but I wanted to believe the good I saw in her. Our friendship dated back to my days in the basement. We both came from absolutely nothing and made it to LA chasing our dreams.

If "real recognize real," then fake gravitates toward fake. Real and fake people don't speak the same language, so I figured if you fucked with someone like her, then you were no different. You lucked up! I couldn't hide my energy towards Eliza the opportunist, which led to me shutting her out of my life. It was easier for me to cut our relationship off cold-turkey because she was one of those people that can make you forget why she wasn't trustworthy. I had a soft spot for her and silence was the only way I knew how to deal with my anger.

I sat on the balcony late one night in my round chair with a fuzzy blanket, trying to find the stars in the California sky. The slathered city lights made it hard to enjoy the calm but being on the seventh floor helped. I prayed to God to send me my soulmate. The thought of finding the person I was meant to spend my life with brought tears to my eyes. There wasn't any guy in my phone who I felt fit the bill; nobody was ready to settle and build.

The next evening, I got an actual phone call which, timing wise, had me a bit spooked. I didn't answer but decided to FaceTime my aunt to pick her brain. I sent her a screenshot of your profile to get a second opinion. I didn't know if you were gay or just really pretty and into yourself. She responded after viewing a few of your pictures with, "What is there not to like?" I never typically invested too much in anyone's opinion when it came to dating, but my aunt always provided a very different perspective. She just gave me the thumbs-up to do what I really wanted to do.

I called you back as soon as I got off the phone with her. We chatted on the phone for three hours. I couldn't even tell you the last time a person had me walking around smiling doing random things while talking on the phone. It brought back high school memories of sneaking to the closet to talk to your crush late in the night when you were supposed to be in bed. I actually did that once. I was in 10th grade on the phone with someone's boyfriend who I had no business talking to, but we would walk to Spanish class together and make out in the hallway. It didn't take long for my grandma to overhear me and bust me out all loud, completely embarrassing me. I loved that woman.

Besides my first boyfriend, Seth, I hadn't exactly been dating "regular" guys. My logic has always been, "Go big or go home," so most of the guys I was linked to were top-tier in their professions. A lot of it had to do with my ego because I knew if I wasn't in the position I was in, they would have never looked my way. I had the "new rapper, new money" complex. Everything I couldn't have before was now mine for the taking. The opportunities became infinite. It's not that I ever wanted anything from these men, but knowing they had shit to lose made me feel more comfortable dealing with them. Death could happen in the blink of an eye, so why not fuck every guy I ever fantasized about having?

I came to the conclusion that maybe that was my problem. I was too focused on the shell of a person rather than who they really were on the inside. Maybe I just needed someone who had potential without all the drama that came with money, fame, and women ready to suck and fuck at the drop of a hat.

You had a big-boy career making peanuts, but it was respectable, I saw the vision. I made six times more than what you made monthly, and we were both aware of that. I was prepared to put up my money if it meant making this work. You didn't have enough financial cushion to afford me, but the way you challenged me mentally was priceless. Every conversation with you ended with me gushing over you from the mental stimulation. You even turned me onto politics. Watching these news channels felt like reality television without the drink-throwing. You taught me new words and gave me assignments on topics to read about for our conversation the next day. You were impressed at how well I was able to explain the Israeli-Palestinian conflict after I did minimal research.

We wanted to meet in person to confirm what we both were feeling was real. You offered to go half on a plane ticket, but in my mind, that didn't give me any greater incentive. I appreciated the gesture more than I expected to see the money back. Relationships are give-and-take, right? Why do all the responsibilities traditionally fall back on the man when women are equally as powerful? I didn't want to leave room for anyone to wonder what I brought to the table when it was clear I bought the damn table.

I was counting down the days to see you like it was Christmas. You were still going to be at work when I landed, but I was fine with that since I could use that time to do my hair and makeup. That morning, you sent a thorough message that listed your address, gate code, where you put my towel, and the room temperature water if I preferred it. I walked into CNN playing in the background because you didn't like the eeriness of a quiet house. The inside looked like a page straight from a magazine. You definitely had the help of a woman, who I later learned was your mother.

I left my luggage and things near the door as I took in my surroundings. I gave myself a tour to learn more about the man who was living here. I made my way back downstairs and decided to get ready in that bathroom so I could lay out all my stuff. Getting ready is like surgery – it's tedious, messy, and time-consuming. I didn't want it to feel like there was a woman in your space even though there was. Once I located the broom, I didn't feel guilty about getting my hair everywhere. I had a few hours before I made my grand first impression.

As soon as I got everything laid out, I heard the garage door opening. I was in a frenzy trying to decide my next move, with my edges resembling a Brillo pad and no eyebrows on my face. I pulled my shirt over my head and peeked my head out just as you closed the door to the garage. You read the bewilderment written all over my face and explained you got off work early so we could spend more time together. Inside, I was flattered by you doing that for me, all while just seconds from having a nervous breakdown. I didn't feel my sexiest by any means but I just went up to you and kissed you. I know you had to be thinking, *damn this bitch was ready for me, waiting at the door!* Men underestimate the power of conversation. If a man has a woman's mind, he has her pussy leaking without saying a word. Sex was a make-or-break ordeal for me after being so sexually neglected in my relationship with Seth. Call it what you want, but if the dick was going to be disappointing, I would rather find out sooner than later before getting in too deep.

Everything unraveled like a scene from a porno. Your aura oozed with the type of confidence that only came from a man who knew what the fuck he was doing. Well, you certainly didn't disappoint me, to say the least! I was relieved we got that out of the way. I know the person reading might see my way of thinking as backwards, but what is normal for the spider is chaos for the fly. Life is about perspective; I just have a direct approach about it.

I didn't want those few days with you to end. You got me out of my food comfort zone and had me enjoying things I would've never tried on my own. Your spontaneity made me realize how much I lacked it. Where I was the dreamer, you were more analytical. Before I knew it, I was on my flight home back to reality. A couple days later on a FaceTime call, you asked me what I would've done if a girl had come down the stairs when I first arrived. You posed this hypothetical as a way of seeing where my mind was with everything. It was too early to be feeling possessive, but I did. I could've downplayed my feelings, but I didn't. If my not wanting you to be with anyone else made me crazy, then I was crazy. Sue me, I'm human. Playing an honest hand is always worth the gamble, because either way it pans out, you never walk away a loser.

I told you I would've been upset, but ultimately, I would have left you alone. I didn't have any desire to knowingly or unknowingly compete for any man's companionship. If I wanted to sign up for misery, I might as well set my price and cry in a Bentley. I was interested in you because I believed that if a man had less, he would see me as more. You told me you knew I viewed casual sex like a guy, and you didn't want to share me either. I had tunnel vision to a fault when it was regarding someone I cared about that way. I would find myself in these imaginary relationships without requiring any real commitment, and I learned the downside to that mentality the hard way. Moving forward, I told myself that "no exclusivity" meant no rules. I had to teach myself to be ruthless to survive regardless of how empty it made me feel. You responded by saying that what we were describing was a relationship, so if we were going to do it, let's do it right. We made it official that day.

I was stunned. I couldn't believe I just got myself into a full-blown relationship that easily. I had so many loose ends to tie with men that no woman in her right mind would ever ignore. What would be the reaction on social media? Would people still care enough to follow me? Did their support run deeper than my relationship status or was it the end to a fantasy? I had been single for years but had experienced several gut-wrenching breakups during that time. How was I going to tell my family, my friends, or the Internet? Did it always happen this fast when it was real? Shouldn't I be happy a guy wanted to claim me after being continuously dogged out? Will I be more respected now that I had a man to validate I wasn't as crazy as everyone made me out to be? With all these questions, I couldn't help but marvel at being your first official girlfriend. It was pretty pathetic how much I convinced myself that you were some savior.

We flaunted our union in the most obnoxious way and people still called it "#goals." Every guy I ever had an open dialogue with watched my Snapchat post at some point but never reached out. I knew it was going to be a pain in the ass getting back in their good graces, but it was worth it for you. We helped one another grow in different areas, which was more than what some of them could say. I was proud to be with you.

You gained a lot of attention in a short amount of time from having me on your arm. You had been with other known Instagram girls, but I put you on. Nobody was checking for you until they saw you checking in with me. A lot of people were rooting for my happiness, but not with you. You tried to pass off being self-absorbed as misunderstood and confident. Truthfully, you were trying to overcompensate for having low self-esteem. I ignored whatever aspects of you I didn't like, just how I ignored the little voice in my head that tried to sway me from doing unnecessarily dumb shit. They just didn't know you like I knew you; they couldn't see what I saw.

We lived in very different worlds doing very different things. You went to work and I woke up to create. I was more than willing to help you in whatever way I could. You wanted more followers but never posted enough to be worth the follow. When I came into town, we planned "picture days" when you'd bring a few outfits to shoot in with me as your personal photographer. Your goal was to get to 100K, and I wanted to make that happen for you. And why would I not want what you wanted for yourself? Who better? I wanted my man to get his shine on too.

There was nothing I wanted to change about you, but could you say the same? I brushed it off when you made a comment about my neon-colored fingernails being ugly and childish. You said you preferred light pinks, white or nude. Pause. You made sure to let me know your mother would never be caught dead with the color I chose. Not only was I confused, but I was also holding back the bull who you flashed red. But wait, there's more! You then followed up with what I should and shouldn't be eating because, evidently, you were a health expert.

Triggers are a funny thing especially when you haven't made any effort towards healing because you didn't know there was anything left to heal. Seth used to police our diets so much that I cringed at the thought of ever monitoring what I ate that heavily again. I know every vegan or bodybuilder reading found that statement repulsive. I wanted to enjoy my life in all areas, and that included food. I hated how I allowed him to control me and I wasn't about to make the same mistake with you. We go into our first argument that night, and when I tried to explain the history behind my response, you didn't get it. You couldn't understand how either one of those "trivial" things warranted my behavior. It wasn't a matter of it being trivial to you or not; it was a big deal to me and it made me upset. For the sake of deescalating the situation before it intensified even more, you apologized. I accepted, we hugged, and we continued on with our night. I was so impressed that you, a man, apologized to me instead of calling me names or storming out. I was too focused on you being able to say a simple sorry than I was on the initial reason I was angry in the first place.

At my next nail appointment, I picked out the lightest pink from the vast selection. It was just a nail color, I thought. Maybe I overreacted; I know I can be rather dramatic sometimes. If this simple change was going to make you more attracted to me as a whole, I was willing to do it. When you picked me up from the airport, the first thing you noticed was my fresh manicure. You grabbed my hand in complete shock and kissed it. Instead of standing my ground, I conformed to your liking, only reinforcing the start of more toxic behavior. Nothing was wrong with my nails to begin with; they were just a problem for *you*. It was too early in our relationship to part ways over what could've merely been just a hiccup. I was going to make this work to prove to everyone and myself that I wasn't crazy.

You became more opposed to the type of content I posted on social media. Your logic was that all the girls you knew didn't have to pose or dance the way I did, and they still had followers. I was open to trying new things but you made me feel bad for being myself. You always would say I was more than my ass, but I knew that already. I felt you were trying to prove a point to me, all while making me fit this image of your perfect girl. I could never be perfect even if I dedicated the rest of my life to it. I still tried to change by doing less and wearing more. No guy wants the girl he's dating showing off things he feels belong to him. When you talk to a person every day, you learn their schedule and patterns. When something feels off, it usually is. Every inconsistency poses a question. On weekends, our texting varied but that wasn't my issue.

There's nothing more embarrassing than opening a social media app to find out your boyfriend is doing something you don't like. Here you were getting a whole massage at a club, captioning it, "Hands of God." I've never been great at math so help me out here. If you told me I had "Hands of God" and you told the random broad at the club she has "Hands of God," did that mean I didn't have to give you massages anymore? I thought being with a guy the world considered "regular" would turn out to be a better experience than I had previously, but apparently, that was not the case.

You didn't hear from me, which initiated a text message you should've sent hours before when your thumbs decided to post on Snapchat. Being a sarcastic cunt, I replied with "How was Hands of God?" I asked just to watch you figure your own way out. I ignored your predictable clueless response, which then prompted a telephone call. You never had a girlfriend, blah blah blah, you're still learning what's acceptable and what's not, blah blah blah. You don't need a ton of relationship experience to not be an inconsiderate assclown.

You claimed the massage was paid for so it wasn't like that, you shouldn't have to delete the Snap, but you were sorry, etc.

I forgave you because it was trivial, right? If the roles were reversed, it would have been a bigger issue even though for argument's sake, you wouldn't admit that. You should've considered being an attorney. I was cool with teaching you the ropes of Relationships 101 since they didn't teach you that - or common sense - in school. I was happy we were able to communicate like two adults, despite you not really being sorry when even a few of your friends told you it looked shady. It should've been a crime being that cute and convincing.

When you broadcast your relationship, it becomes everyone's business. Even if you try to hide it and people still find out, it becomes everyone's business. I had a DM sent to my inbox with a picture of two girls attached, girls I had never seen in my life, taking a mirror selfie in your house. You never mentioned you were having guests over that weekend. The last text I got from you said you were playing video games and relaxing. They wanted it to be known that they were in the house of my boyfriend who allegedly appeared happy as a clam with me. Every girl knows what they're doing when they make a point to show you their location. It's always done on purpose because girls want you to know that shit ain't as sweet as you may think.

If you wouldn't want it done to you, it's safe to assume you probably shouldn't do it to someone with whom you supposedly share feelings. I can admit that with every incident, I wasn't always able to use the words or tone needed to keep the conversation progressive towards finding a solution. You said if I made a habit out of responding to problems in a negative manner, then the relationship wasn't going to work. Funny enough, I never blew up, never name-called, and never even yelled. I respected you, but I had no problem with calling you out. Even funnier, you were the one who told your friend Rod during a night out dining that you liked how I didn't let you get away with bullshit - hence, admitting you'd tried in the past and failed.

When I called you about the mirror selfie, I was very accusatory. I couldn't wrap my mind around all the careless incidents when they could've been avoided. You think I liked playing detective? Getting messages from strangers about my dude? Who wants to fuss about shit all day long, especially if there's a misunderstanding? The two girls were friends who came over so you all could ride together to the kickback since everyone was meeting at the club that night. What could I say, other than I'm sorry for not believing you? I didn't think you were lying because I know I wouldn't lie. I started to feel the miles between us in this long-distance relationship. Maybe I just missed you and was overdue for a visit. I didn't think too much into you living in a city notorious for beautiful women because I wanted to trust you. I just figured you valued building over meaningless girls and sex; that's why we were together, right? If you put us together, *how they gon' stop both of us, right?*

I flew in the next week, giddy to finally see you after a few weeks. You had a lot planned for us, so I was excited to have fun together. Remember the night of your friend's graduation? We slithered throughout that mansion on a mission like Francis and Claire on "House of Cards." Not to mention, my tight little red dress made quite the impression. Almost everyone made a comment about you finally bringing someone to an event since you always came "dolo." You had to mingle and kiss ass with a few people there on whom you wanted to make a good impression, so we split up. I knew this was my opportunity to highlight my people skills and effortless grace when the stakes were high.

I had the women there telling their husbands to refill our drinks while we took selfies down by the ocean. I had the best white-person-pretending-to-listen face and knew the importance of an ego fluff. When you came back, I could see a look in your eyes that told me everything I already knew. You were impressed. You had nothing to fear. I was safe to bring around the big bad scary white people from work. I could adapt to any environment. You said I passed your test since these gatherings were frequent, but to me, that was light work. I wanted you to recognize my value.

It struck me as odd when we only had sex once out of the few days I was there. We hadn't seen each other in weeks and you were acting as if I lived right down the street. I thought this was the time to be sex-crazed and all over one another, but I suppose not. Instead, we watched basketball, bet on games, and at one point, were folding clothes together. Maybe we were transitioning? Was this normal? I felt more like one of the guys than your actual girlfriend. Something wasn't right.

I caught my flight back home and later went out to dinner with my aunt to express my concerns. Was I crazy? Was I overthinking? Was I trying to sabotage a good thing? Maybe I wasn't giving you a fair chance. I knew in my gut that I didn't want to be with you just based on it being more stressful than it was fun. I didn't want to randomly break things off without having a conversation first. I should've trusted my instincts, but I was hoping you'd prove me wrong.

When we FaceTimed later that night, I came straight out and asked why we didn't have sex more often. You said it was deeper than sex so it wasn't something you were pressed to do. Your answer was cute, but I had needs too. You further explained that you felt a lot of pressure to always perform well and my being a "sex zombie" was intimidating. I could appreciate your transparency, but it wasn't good enough for me. When we talked the next day, it felt forced. I didn't feel bad about being upfront, but I was sure to be sensitive to your feelings. No man wants to feel like he's not doing his job…especially being miles away.

I have always been an extremely family-oriented person with homebody tendencies, while you would be fiending to go out on the weekends. I could've spent the 4th of July with you but choosing you over my family was blasphemous. We started off normal but when I asked you about your plans, I didn't hear from you all day. You had no problem posting your whereabouts on Snapchat, but I wasn't worthy of a text back. Whenever you think you're being ignored, it's because you usually are.

Thank God your fingers weren't broken; you were just

shirtless on a boat full of bitches. You made it obvious you missed the freedoms you had when you were single. Of course, having women with little-to-no substance as entertainment for a couple guys was way cooler than spending quality time with a person you actually care about. I didn't get angry or send any threatening texts because logic paints the picture emotions tend to distort. The answer is in the question itself when you think about it.

I finally got a FaceTime call from you at 11:50pm, and you couldn't even fake like you were the least bit thrilled to be talking to me. Several awkward silences later, I couldn't hold back what was on my heart. I asked you was this not something you wanted anymore because your patterns not only made me feel like a burden but also were hurtful.

Too many times, we as women underestimate our ability pick up on the subtle emotional messages being sent by others. Our emotions often cloud our judgment, but when we are willing to seek the truth, we always find what we already knew. We *choose* what we want to see just as we *choose* what we want to overlook. Have you ever heard of men's intuition? Me neither.

I held off for weeks, Solomon, because I believed in you. I wanted to give you the benefit of the doubt, but sadly, you just proved me right. I thought with our powers combined, we could be an unstoppable force. Not a lot of people know your background or that the moniker you use isn't even your government name. Your name-brand clothes, shoes, suits, jewelry, house, and car... your parents paid for those things.

You told me you weren't considered attractive throughout your formative years, which would explain how you developed the ugly duckling syndrome. Even when you blossomed, you thought you were never good enough. You wanted to "fuck the same girls all the famous guys did" so you could feel like you were on their level. Confidence can be faked; self-esteem…not so much. You knew the truth behind your façade, which is why you had to overcompensate.

I was a conquest. Being with me had nothing to do with me as a person, but more so what I represented in your mind. Take a desirable girl, make her yours, and boom - you're the man. The only problem with being an opportunist is that what makes the person you're attempting to leech off special doesn't make *you* special. It's not because you're not special, but because you're not walking in your own path, which is what ultimately differentiates you. You can attend every party and pose in every photo, but being relevant by association is just that. Serves me right, trying to change for a man. There was nothing wrong with the way I was. I wasn't some horse you could break down and ride whenever you pleased. I was meant to run wild, and it took experiencing this relationship to see my inner power.

People who appear to be intelligent can be clueless too. The thought of you using me like a 90-day-trial run made it easy to think how easily I could've painted the roses red by splattering your brain across the cabinets with the gun you kept under the island in the kitchen. I guess we both dodged a bullet, huh? You're welcome.

HECTOR
Dancing With The Devil

I had been plugging in different variables in this love equation but kept getting the same result. Being a good-hearted person wasn't good enough. To be "good" was to be taken advantage of and taken for granted. As much as guys say women don't want the nice guy, it stands just as true for men not wanting the nice girl. Guys want the woman society defines as worthy of being a wife regardless of whether it's what they really want. Guys want the woman who is the easiest to manage, the one they can come home to only to cheat on them with the bad girls. These are the bad girls who "act out" because they aren't seen as good enough for much else. If you're going to play the role, play it well, right?

For months, I tried to convince Solomon that I was this good girl when I knew I was only kidding myself. It's not that my heart is not pure, but I indulge in too many things and attitudes that align me with the bad girls. I am not just good or bad, I am a walking paradox. I am beautiful and terrifying like the weather. Uncontainable and mysterious like the ocean, but if one were to dive in, they would see how the depth of my beauty surpasses the surface. I am everything because I know no limits. A true goddess knows she is peace as much as she is capable of war. Kind, yet wrathful; soft, but tough; like Heaven and Hell in human form.

Why did I have to fit an image to be accepted? What was wrong with me just being myself? I felt my discouragement grow into a bitter rage, knowing that these men were not looking in me, but looking *at* me. They could not get past my outer layer to see the radiance my heart emitted. Seeing is believing, and the more you believe, the more you are able to see. I felt banished from the kingdom of love so much that my heart began to blacken like fog spreading on an eerie night. I was the villain, even when I wasn't, but became the dark part of a vengeful queen.

Solomon wanted to be "friends" after our split, but being an all-in or all-out type of bitch, I coldly rejected the moronic idea of it. People are only capable of wearing the mask for so long before you catch them without it. We are deceived by the illusions of what we wish to see rather than seeing things as they truly are. Ideals are deeply embedded in our hearts from the things we did or didn't have growing up. *Why?* It only hurts more in the end.

Last, but certainly not least, my dearest Hector. We had each other's number for a year and some change, but our relationship only consisted of random texts and unscheduled FaceTime appointments. You were the furthest thing from my type, but your eyes told a different story. You were soft-spoken but always had this way of making me laugh in the most unexpected way. We were friends and that's what I needed at that time.

Shortly after my split from Solomon, I made swift efforts to move on as the Queen of Like It Never Happened would. You invited me to come to your event in New Orleans, assuring me there were no expectations - just two people finally getting the opportunity to meet. My aunt saw my eagerness as alarming but didn't impose her opinion one way or another. She knew I was always going to follow my heart even if it came off utterly mad. Since the nature of it never touched the rim of being sexual I felt comfortable with my last minute decision.

When you picked me from the airport and I hopped in the sprinter, I couldn't believe I actually came. The majority of our harsh society saw you as grotesque and odd, but your colorful aura was warm like a cloudless day. We were polar opposites and that's what captivated me the most. You said our union made you feel like the nerdy underdog that bagged the popular cheerleader all the jocks wanted. Two misunderstood rebels the world saw as villains, united fighting the same cause. To them, I was a black widow; to you, I was your butterfly.

Before heading out, you gave me a navy blue jewelry box without saying a word. Silly me who never got many gifts thought that I was to hold it for you, so I did. After a few moments and a perplexed look on your face, you told me to open it. Slightly embarrassed, I cracked the box open slowly to the sight of a diamond necklace. As much as people are convinced I value materialistic things, I have never been materialistic. Growing up relatively poor and knowing the importance of investing in my brand, I never formed expensive habits.

I knew this was from your heart and that's what made it special to me. You made me feel special; I wasn't used to that.

The more time we spent together, the more we became attached. It's as if our hearts hugged tightly in the relief of knowing the same pain. The first time we kissed, it happened mid-conversation; we just went for it. After the first time we had sex I wanted more because I wanted all of you. From cordial encounters to a looming magnetic obsession, the idea of loving you was exhilarating.

There was one day I sucked your dick six times. I swallowed your kids twice before noon, I call that a Champion's Breakfast. I could've cared less about the next time we'd fuck because I was too fixated on sucking what was left of your soul. Your demonic seeds danced down my throat and formed a Conga line to my belly. Who needed drugs when the thought of what was to sprout had yet to come?

Our upbringings were almost too different to share similarities, but we related in its dysfunction. We talked about the gift and curse of the life we chose where people all over knew our names. Your carefree spirit could make any person abandon their daily responsibilities. You were fearless without a worry of tomorrow, and I wanted to find that place. In the words of Marshall Mathers, "I was at a fork in the road and took the psychopath."

When you removed our shells, we were just two empty people who wanted a love that would never leave. You had been mistreated and lied to like me. We both had an infinite amount of love to give. You would throw a fit like a toddler who didn't get his way when it was time for me to go home. You wanted me to stay on the road with you and travel but your money wasn't mine; I had to stay focused. I would have run away with you if I could've, but my mind wouldn't let me make that mistake again.

The next time I saw you and we had sex, you hit it while wearing your inverted chain on I didn't like. When we were done, I told you the things it represented were nothing to play with. You chuckled and said, "I wore it on purpose. If I had sex with you with it on, what does that make you? You're no better." As fucked up as that sounds when I replay it back in my mind, you were absolutely right. I was as good as wearing the damn thing myself. Somehow, this realization drew me in closer to you, closer to the darkness.

If we were nothing alike, where was the common denominator? Individually, we were strange and unusual, but together, even more strange and unusual. The people who thought we had no business being together based on our physical appearances alone didn't know us. If they saw you as Lucifer's equivalent, then I was playing devil's advocate. I wasn't innocent enough to be worthy of a husband but was too innocent to be seen with the likes of you? If I was such a saint, how could we relate? Maybe my angelic heart saw things the average heart simply couldn't see. Like draws like; it doesn't have a particular face.

What I loved the most about you was the fact that you seemed to accept me for me. You were the first guy to applaud me for running wild in the wind. What was off-putting to so many before you, you saw as dope. You gave me a piece of advice that completely changed the trajectory of my life. I was on the fence about fitting an idea or being my ideas; I was imprisoned by the potential judgment of others I'd face if I took off my mask. It was written for me to meet you because I was meant to live a life without being confined to an identity that wasn't mine. You helped me see the uniqueness of the individuality I had all along.

You had more unfinished business on your side than I was fully aware of. Women were making themselves known due to the intimidation of my relevance in your life. I hated that I was even mentioned in the same sentence with girls you swore never held a candle to me. You grouped them as "little bitches" and emphasized that I reigned far above that category. You couldn't draw a single comparison, yet you never erased them in fear of us not working out. You put your ex on the map and she still lied, so I understood your uneasiness.

My ego wouldn't let it fly, or my common sense. I told you and myself I was done with you until you had something logical to say. Those few days of no communication ate at me and caused me to break down an explanation of my silence too thoroughly, even though I did nothing wrong. I wanted to fix this; I wanted to fix *you*. Your response brought me to tears when you told me you loved me for the first time. As much as I wanted to stay mad at you, I felt the same way about you.

There wasn't a whole lot of substance to our relationship, but oddly enough, we discussed having a kid together. You told me your life was moving fast but you were moving faster to get all the things you wanted out of it. I pondered the possibilities of a future together and what our child would be like, but I never took you seriously. After the third time of you mentioning me getting in vitro to have your first son, I knew this was something you were seriously considering. I remember being speechless on the other end of our call, but I couldn't help feeling secretly eager. Before you hung up, you reminded me to start thinking of a name. My mind went into mania. This contradicted everything I dreamed my first pregnancy to be, but for you, I was down. I had thought at this age, I would have found someone and had at least one child, but life never really goes as you plan it.

I asked my hairstylist, Curt, his opinion on the idea of me getting pregnant, and he responded with, "What in your life is missing that you feel the need to have a baby?" Even though he had no clue who I was referring to, his question touched on an internal battle I was avoiding. I noticed as I got older, I began to suppress my hidden desires to have a family in fear of never having one. Who wouldn't want an Alien rock star dad and down-to-earth mom? I didn't know what people would think, but it couldn't have been any worse than what they already did.

What I saw as entering a new chapter was the beginning of the end. You came to LA and stood me up three nights in a row. It wouldn't have been so bad if I wasn't sitting on the couch dressed and ready each night. There I sat in the dark, a hopeful romantic that had hoped with all the wrong people. You were too high to give a fuck, which explained your limited replies, pitiful excuses, and your disregard of the concept of time. You treated me like I was nothing to you. You treated me like I was the freak the world turned their nose up at time and time again. I thought I was being understanding, but it was just you abusing my kindness.

Was I a professional doormat? Was I that desperate for love? I was always there for you and you can never fucking deny that. I gave you the benefit of the doubt despite your constant efforts to eat away at what made our bond special. Me being me, I gave you another shot. On the fourth night, you came through. You told me to be ready at 9pm but didn't pull up till 12:30am. I had to be up early in the morning, but a little sleep deprivation was worth it to spend time with you.

I hated how you made me feel on a regular basis but loved you too much to give up. After I left in the morning to make my class, I texted you saying how I had a great time and hoped to see you a few more times while you were in town. I never heard back from you the remainder of the time you were here. I learned that no response is a response. By the time I had typed my overly lengthy text you wouldn't have given two shits about, you were on a flight to the next city. Nothing mattered to you outside of you. You never touched me after the second we had sex in months of being involved. If I stopped giving you head, there would be no intimacy. Another tale for the books with a selfish piece of shit.

I got a text that night from a friend who attached a birthday invitation that no person in their right mind would refuse. As harmless as it was, I knew my attendance would destroy everything between us. I called my aunt, trying to justify the idea of not going to the party, but she warned me I'd be stupid not to go. It's not like we were together Hector, your actions spoke loud enough for you.

I ended up going and **nothing was the same** after that. You sent the "Hope you're having fun" text that every guy sends who is too frightened to act like he gives a damn about a girl he gives a damn about. I can't say it was "too little, too late," because you never cared enough from the start. It just gave you every excuse not to trust me and strengthened your argument of me not really liking you. You never wanted to believe I could really like you for you because you weren't looking into me, just *at* me.

Men protect their egos at all costs for fear of you seeing them vulnerable. We as women want equality but place men in a one-size-fits-all "be a man" box. Life is about balance, and that includes the feminine energy all men typically are taught to lock away. Gender aside, you will regret the feelings you didn't act upon due to your own ego. It is your own worst enemy because it is never on your side for your greater good. It took one party to obliterate what we had.

I so terribly wanted to feel some form of remorse, but I didn't. The evil seeds I had growing inside me grew to be a bush of thorny little monsters. The amount of hatred I had pumping throughout my body only fueled their increasing size. The windows to my soul beamed with a vacancy I couldn't switch off. I was happy you were hurting; you had nobody to blame but your fucking self.

Despite you being different, you were no different. You wouldn't know a good thing even if that good thing was holding you like a baby in the studio until 9am. I don't give a fuck how insane I sound for caring about you, because I did. I paid a pretty price for all the ugly those bitches put you through. For someone who claims to this day to have never judged me, you judged me. You judged me based on my appearance, just like so many did to you. You never gave me a real chance to show you that not all girls are the same. When you don't want anything from a person, it's easy to like them for who they really are because they're not needed for survival. Wanting someone is a choice, whereas needing someone is temporary and conditional. Most of the time when a person needs you, they rarely want you in the end once they've exhausted what initially made you valuable. I liked you more than you'll ever know...until now, I guess.

You were my muse, Hector. The impact you had on my life helped to awaken creativity I didn't even know I possessed. I discovered the things human beings are most ashamed of; our darkness - the masks we wear - is where the true hidden treasure lies buried hoping we answer our own riddle to unlock it. If too much sunlight is a desert, then the absence of sunlight is death. Balance requires the acknowledgment of the necessity of both, for they are not to be limited to being seen as good or bad. A dense mind will never know the freedoms of being able to perceive any given situation from an array of perspectives at will. I learned that I could love anyone because I learned to love myself. They say opposites attract, but maybe you were put in my life to send me in the opposite direction.

CLOSING

We are taught to bully the differences we see in others as they pose threat to our glorified ignorance. You have to question everything in a society that chastises free thinkers but rewards the sheeple for abiding by the rules. *Good monkey gets banana, bad monkey no banana.* No human walking God's green Earth is licensed to disrespect, degrade, or discredit one's right to be different. Our appearance, qualities, and experiences are what make each of our stories one of a kind. I wish we would all share them more; maybe then we would see we're not so different from each other after all. To police creativity instead of nurturing it and teaching those how to use it, is not only a society being set up for failure but for mass genocide. We fear what we don't know because we don't take the time to understand. Right is a direction, wrong is subjective.

The happiness is in the hardships, the lessons are in the irony of those hardships. When you know of great sorrow, you will never be a stranger to great happiness. Why do we fantasize about the finish line when the gems are along the journey? We get so caught up in how accomplishments appear on paper when being happy is the only goal of importance to pursue relentlessly.

The sexiest you'll feel is when you can be comfortable just being yourself. Material items, your relationship status, how many followers you have, or what's in your bank account will never fill the voids in your heart. How are you wishing to be someone else when the version of yourself you aspire to be is at the tip of your fingers, in the thoughts that flood your subconscious, and in your ability to never stop dreaming? Do you believe in magic?

When dealing with monsters, you have to fight like hell not to become a monster. You can run, but the monsters know every place you will hide. Sometimes the monster lying next to you in bed becomes the monsters now residing in your head. Hurt people hurt people, and if after being hurt you decide to hurt people, you are no better than the hurt people. When we are at our angriest, it's no coincidence to be on the verge of tears. The short temper you think you have is just the cause and effect of not tending to what is going on under the circus tent. You must run towards the darkness to find your salvation. How can your demons haunt you if you are bold enough to stand in their presence and steal a hug? Your demons are what trying to escape a Haunted House symbolizes. Every room represents your illusions designed to deter you from growth with hopes you will run in fear. As you start to see things for what they are, unafraid, you advance deeper to your final test. Behind the last door, your traumas wait to greet you with a smile and shame. Can you handle confronting what has held you hostage? You don't need heavy machinery to defeat them when you are your own weapon of mass infinitive power. The monsters cannot win without your help. If you were to know your strength, they'd lose control; that's why they make living in your truth so painful. It is time to take control of your life and start living the life you know you're capable of creating. In "The Matrix," Morpheus said, "There is a difference between knowing the path and walking the path."

It took me years to find my voice I gave away so carelessly like Ariel did Ursula over a prince who didn't care that she was a mute. I was practicing my roar as young Simba did, not knowing everything would come crashing down once I realized my Queen within. New levels bring new devils. The monsters will always want back in. Lying is easy but it gets you nowhere; hence, the truth being the greatest gift you can give to yourself and others. There was nothing my family, friends, or any religion could've done to save me from me. It takes getting to a certain point on your own to start questioning the worth of living in fear and being consistently mistreated.

I've been the side bitch, the main bitch, the one-of-many bitch, the naive bitch, the here-let-me-fix-it bitch, but a bitch that never believed she deserved to be more than some bitch to some guy. I was content being second best because I didn't feel worthy of first. Fighting for any man or woman to love you is not a love reciprocated. Wounds heal in the presence of love; love doesn't try to tear you apart for personal gain. How can you say it's love with conviction if it is impatient, unkind, envious, boastful, proud, rude, self-seeking, easily angered, keeps a record of wrongs, delights in evil, repulsed by truth, never protects, never trusts, and never hopes or perseveres? What the fuck kind of love are you on? You are worthy of the love you dream of because if you can dream it, anything can happen. You know why? The love meant for you would never have you pulling your hair out searching for it because it would never want your heart to be troubled or think the answers are outside of you.

If you try to raise your standards, you're asking for too much or being unrealistic. If you're guarded, you're jaded. God forbid you actually have a backbone and call a man out on something - now you're the crazy one. You'll never win with the wrong people. What they really want you to do is to raise your tolerance for their fuckery. I know a lot of phenomenal men and women that aren't married, but I also know plenty of married couples who allow themselves to be blatantly disrespected for the sake a title. The assumption is that something has to be wrong with single people while being miserable in a relationship is completely normalized.

Men will step their shit up when we leave them with no other option but to step their shit up. Have you ever applied to Harvard? No? Me neither. Why? I know damn well I don't fit their criteria, so I would never waste my time applying to their school. Think of your heart, mind, and pussy like Harvard. Many will come but few are chosen. You can't afford to waste a second of your time on a student who didn't even follow the application properly. Weed them out early; you are worth the wait and will thank me later. Don't sit around idealizing like I did and end up missing the red flags. I was impatient and lowered my requirements to increase the number of potential applicants. I thought if I made it easier to get in, it would be easier for a man to love me. I shortchanged my worth and wondered why I came out feeling cheated.

There is no room for doubt when a goddess understands she has been a goddess all along. She laughs in the face of adversity, masturbates to the thought of uncertainty, and trusts the reality she is constantly creating with her thoughts. When I was at my lowest, life kicked me even harder when I was down. Whenever I felt like I was breaking, I knew I wasn't because I was never made to break to begin with. If I have more to give, I give it everything in the tank. I'm the author of my life, and if I am being put through it, I know I can rewrite my story to see through it.

Life is like a pop quiz. You can either study for hours or not study, banking on the chance that the teacher will forget. You're tested when you're least expecting it because you're least expecting it. Duh! If you don't take it seriously, you will be forced to never forget what you were overlooking. You getting handed that big fat F in red ink isn't a failure if you learned the importance of studying. Our divine purpose is a binder full with blank loose-leaf paper you have to fill with the dreams and aspirations you hold closest to your heart, the ones only you can see.

Every single person is absolutely capable of change, but they rarely do it. Accountability can feel sobering yet excruciating with being exposed to the reality of your reflection. You must hold a mirror to your bullshit, rebuking toxic behaviors and self-destructive thinking. It's saying, "I can make a change starting today. I am not stuck but I must fight for me. I am worth it." Evidence that a person truly wants to change is when their actions match their words. Is it a coincidence some of the biggest manipulators are also the most charming? Words are here today, gone tomorrow; the answers you seek are in the actions.

If you want to move forward, you must retrace your steps back to the very beginning. Back to a time where things were simple because they just were. Being able to flutter your eyes as you begin to stir awake from the night's slumber is enough to want to live your best life. If you believe things happen randomly without rhyme or reason, I wouldn't expect you to appreciate the intricately orchestrated details in this beautiful symphony we're a part of.

You have to make it your duty to be true to yourself and it starts with authenticity. Authenticity is the practice of unlearning all the heavily-distorted, narrow-minded views of what you were told to be, and instead, being who you truly want to be. Perhaps if I did everything I didn't do, I would've never endured and suffered all the things I did. I live a life of no regrets because I know of love and as long as I know love, I am never as lost as I may feel. If you don't follow your heart, take that job, make that move, fight through the fights with irreplaceable people, and give it all you got, you will regret your entire life wishing you did. Calm seas never made a skilled sailor, so you better hold on tight Captain, because it's going to be a bumpy ride! The more you believe, the more you will see that the dreams you wish to come true are just within your grasp. It doesn't hurt that the universe recognizes and supports the efforts of a resilient heart.

When you find yourself dwelling in a negative emotion, remember that change is constant. Allow yourself to feel whatever it is you're feeling, but don't you fucking give up. Everything in the universe is happening <u>for</u> you, not <u>to</u> you. If you don't feel like getting out of bed, then don't. But you crawl out of that motherfucker until you can find the strength in your legs to walk again. I promise you that you'll feel so proud knowing you chose to persevere during the darkest of days. You are never alone, even on the days you feel like nobody would notice if you were gone. YOU WERE PUT ON THIS EARTH TO REMEMBER WHO YOU ARE AND BE YOUR HIGHEST SELF. Your existence was no mistake, honey. Everything in this life is possible.

Corruption goes on behind the doors of churches but from the outside looking in, it's a house of worship. There's a pedophile leading the sermon in the sacred house of the Lord, *did you know that?* Are you sure that was the Holy Ghost you caught? Perception is deception. Nothing is as good as it seems, just like nothing is as bad as it seems because…well, nothing is ever as it seems. How much longer are we going to judge a book by its cover? I'll let you reach your own verdict.

80 ❀ C8